School of Divinity

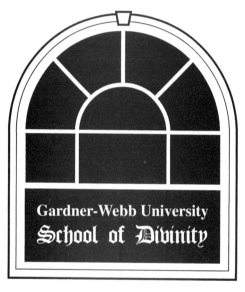

Gardner-Webb University
School of Divinity

This book donated
by

Dr. Tom Steagald

The
Youngest
Day

BY THE AUTHOR

Bed and Board

An Offering of Uncles

The Supper of the Lamb

The Third Peacock

Hunting the Divine Fox

Exit 36

Food for Thought

Party Spirit

A Second Day

Between Noon and Three

THE YOUNGEST DAY

*Shelter Island's Seasons
in the Light of Grace*

Robert Farrar Capon

1817

Harper & Row, Publishers, San Francisco
Cambridge, Hagerstown, New York, Philadelphia
London, Mexico City, São Paulo, Sydney

Grateful acknowledgment is made for the following: quotations on page 146 from *Collected Poems* by Conrad Aiken, reprinted by permission of Oxford University Press; quotations on page 147 from *Collected Poems*, copyright 1921, 1948 by Edna St. Vincent Millay, Harper & Row, Publishers, Inc.

FIRST EDITION

Designed by Donna Davis

Library of Congress Cataloging in Publication Data

Capon, Robert Farrar.

THE YOUNGEST DAY

  1. Seasons—Religious aspects—Christianity. 2. Eschatology. 3. Grace (Theology). I. Title.
BT695.5.C36   1983   242   82–48414
ISBN 0–06–061309–2

---

83 84 85 86 87 10 9 8 7 6 5 4 3 2 1

For Valerie

She openeth her mouth with wisdom;
and in her tongue is the law of kindness.

Contents

Introduction   ix

WINTER / DEATH

ONE   The Creek   3
TWO   The Tide   8
THREE   The Call   14
FOUR   The Light   19
FIVE   The Garden   27
SIX   The Egg   33

SPRING / JUDGMENT

SEVEN   The Fix   41
EIGHT   The Hedge   46
NINE   The Clock   54
TEN   The Time   59

SUMMER / HELL

ELEVEN   The Sun   71
TWELVE   The Evening   76
THIRTEEN   The Porch   82
FOURTEEN   The Funeral   90
FIFTEEN   The Damn   95
SIXTEEN   The Refusal   100

FALL / HEAVEN

SEVENTEEN The Imagery 111
EIGHTEEN The Storing 120
NINETEEN The Poignancy 125
TWENTY The Laughter 132

Epilogue 135

INTRODUCTION

A book about the seasons of the year should, like all musings on nature, plot a middle course between reportage and philosophizing. On the one hand, while the world is full of fascinating facts, our understanding is short-changed if we settle for nothing more than description, however poetic. Nature, if it comes from the hand of Anybody more interesting than Mindless Chance, has got to have double meaning at least: creators always tip fascinating hands in their creations. The Someone Responsible for snowflakes, for example, has a charming if ungovernable love of variations on a theme; the Party that made the platypus is not without a sense of humor; the Conceiver of the insect world has an inordinate, if not exactly fathomable, fondness for beetles.

On the other hand, it will not do simply to sally forth in quest of significance. Things are, before all else, themselves; the Magician who fetches them so unnecessarily from the black hat of nothingness—who so effortlessly holds them up by the ears for our admiring view—would seem to be more captivated by who they are than by what they mean.

Accordingly, this book threads a serious if sometimes zany way between the dull reductionism that sees seasons only as meaningless consequences of the earth's accidentally tilted axis and the lofty theologizing that itches to get beyond this world of matter into the realm of meaning alone. And it does so by resolutely admiring and hefting—and poking into and taking pokes at—both territories at once.

An illustration of the method? Well, consider the skewing of the earth's axis of rotation to the plane of its orbit around the sun. How fabulous that by a mere angle of 66° 33', the respective hemispheres should enjoy summer and winter at the same time. How elegantly economical that one such simple device should give us not only four seasons in Altoona and Sydney but four winds as well—and thus at least sixteen weathers for openers alone. How clever of Whoever it may have been to spare us the disastrous climates that would have resulted from dead perpendicular rotation: boiling hot at the equator, 100 below at the poles and a dismal 42 degrees forever in Philadelphia. Blessed therefore be the Appropriate Party (He, She, It or They, as you like—gratitude should take precedence over genderithmetic), from whom comes every good and perfect gift and who mightily and sweetly orders all things.

Another illustration? All right: take this slantingly spun-off earth with its concomitant gift of seasons. Are they not the very stuff of our hope that history might somehow be a purposeful march on the future and not just a dog's pursuit of its tail? How ingenious of the Top-throwing Party to take such a profoundly circular world as this and, simply by tossing it out at an angle, to give its inhabitants a sense of line and thrust. How thoughtful to have provided us, in the annual progress of winter, spring, summer and fall, with all the materials for conceiving a future perennially new. How encouraging to have so constant a suggestion that we are up to something more directional than sniffing our way around the same old lamppole. Blessed again therefore be the Provident Party who brings forth bread from the earth and wine that makes glad the heart of man—and who wills that seedtime and harvest, and cold and heat, and summer and winter, and day and night shall not cease.

But enough. The subject at hand is the four seasons and the four last things—earth's hints of history and the final future of history itself. Winter is Death, Spring is Judgment, Summer is Hell and Fall is Heaven; and the Grace that reconciles the world is the theme that unites them all. If you wonder about the suitability of taking on nine such topics in one brief pass, wonder no more. Better minds than mine have done it before, and in smaller compass at that. Let me end this preface with the best introduction of all: three sentences from a sermon preached by John Donne—at St. Paul's, Christmas Day in the evening, 1624.

God made Sun and Moon to distinguish seasons, and day and night, and we cannot have the fruits of the earth but in their season: But God hath made no decree to distinguish the seasons of his mercies; In paradise, the fruits were ripe, the first minute, and in heaven it is alwaies Autumne, his mercies are ever in their maturity. We ask *panem quotidianam,* our daily bread, and God never sayes you should have come yesterday, he never sayes you must againe tomorrow, *but to day if you will heare his voice,* to day he will heare you. If some King of the earth have so large an extent of Dominion, in North, and South, as that he hath Winter and Summer together in his Dominions, so large an extent East and West, as that he hath day and night together in his Dominions, much more hath God mercy and judgment together: He brought light out of darknesse, not out of a lesser light; he can bring thy Summer out of Winter, though thou have no Spring; though in the wayes of fortune, or understanding, or conscience, thou have been benighted till now, wintred and frozen, clouded and eclypsed, damped and benummed, smothered and stupefied till now, now God comes to thee, not as in the dawning of the day, not as in the bud of the spring, but as the Sun at noon to illustrate all shadowes, as the sheaves in harvest, to fill all penuries, all occasions invite his mercies, and and all times are his seasons.

ROBERT FARRAR CAPON

Shelter Island, New York
August 1982

WINTER

—

DEATH

one

THE CREEK

It's a cold January morning: about 20 degrees, to judge from the tight curl and perpendicular droop of the rhododendron leaves. After five years on this island I'm finally beginning to judge weather, time and distance without instruments. Rhododendrons, for example, set their leaves just above horizontal at 60 degrees and they lower them progressively as the temperature falls until at 20 degrees they're pretty much straight up and down. That pleases me. I dress for my run not by the radio but by looking out the window at a bush. That, and by checking the sway of the trees to add a rough windchill factor.

It doesn't hurt of course to have a thermometer. The rhododendron leaves, having shot their indicative wad by arriving at right angles to the ground, make no distinction between 20 above and 20 below. Still though, I try not to check the mercury. I walk a circuit of the house, breathing with my mouth open: when my beard doesn't ice up, it's above 10; when it freezes fast, it's closer to zero. If I'm dressed too lightly I go back in and add another layer.

In any case, I have arrived this morning at my first stopping point: a small, two-lane concrete bridge over a tidal creek. The wind is out of the northwest at about twenty knots so I climb down the bank and sit in the lee of the bridge abutment looking up into the marsh. It's been 20 or less here for a week. The ice that edges the creek has been up and down with the tide all that time; now, at low water and with the rising sun just beginning to reach it, it lies in bent, gleaming sheets over the hummocks on the bottom. The ice in my beard, since I'm out of the wind, melts.

Finally I'm warm enough to think about something other than being warm enough so I let my mind watch the creek and flow with it. Till I lived here, I never thought much about the effect of the seasons below the surface of the water. What we can't see, we relegate to mystery. But then we do something foolish. We assume that the mysterious is somehow monochrome—that it has a homogenized, undifferentiated structure—as if there were always fish and always the same kinds and sizes of fish in the creek, the same underwater plants at the same stages of development, the same tides, the same currents, the same bottom.

But none of that is true. The sub-marine seasons are just as varied as the sublunary ones. Not that it takes much observation to see them; just that the prejudice of their nonexistence is so strong we fail to observe.

Fish come and go here, spawning in the spring, growing through summer and fall. Seaweeds and marsh grasses change all the time. Even the phragmites at the sweetwater edge of the marsh—the tall squirrel tails that seem always to be there—are hardly the same two days in a row.

I think back to spring: some small boys standing on this bridge fishing (read, hoping) for flounders. I kid them. Lucky thing, I say, that nature makes creeks flow right under bridges, otherwise they'd be dropping their lines on dry ground. They look at me blankly so I press the point. Didn't they ever think about the wonders of nature? Look at those waterlines on the abutment. Know what they're from? Islands float, I tell them. In the winter, when there are only about a thousand people here on Shelter Island, it rides high in the water. In the summer, when there are fifteen thousand on weekends, it sinks to the high water mark. One boy informs me the mark is only because of the tide. I say, oh, and rub my beard.

The word "only" peeves me. Budding little reductionist! Even if it is the tide, where does he get off assuming that's less fabulous than my fable? Probably grow up to be a sociologist or a used-car salesman or some other species of village sceptic. I decide to fight fire with fire.

See those little white things out in the harbor, I ask. What, he asks back, the buoys? They're not buoys, I tell him; they're boat buds. You just watch. Right now there's not a craft in the harbor, but a couple more weeks of spring and they'll start to sprout: little boats first; then, come Memorial Day, sloops, yawls, ketches, schooners. And if you come down on the Fourth of July you'll see them blossom—great big triangular petals.

My friend says he supposes that on Labor Day they begin to wither and die, huh? I congratulate him. Maybe he won't grow up bad after all. So what if he thinks he's being smart? He's got at least the beginnings of a mind that's open to more than one way of looking at causality. Beats the attitude of walking up to things and telling them in advance what they're doing. I ask him where he supposes they take the boats when they harvest them. That's easy, he says. The fanciest ones they store in boat barns—like the big red one over in Port of Egypt. The crummy ones get left out in yards like culls around a potato shed. He smiles at the simile. This boy may even end up human.

I never did get to use the other lesson I thought up for him. In September when the snappers are running, the fishing off this bridge is more promising. Snappers—young bluefish—are as voracious as big ones and just as clever. They hang in the water under the bridge on a falling tide and wait for the shiners to be carried out. If, while the fisherfish are slashing through their free lunch, a fisherkid drops a baited hook into the melee, he can hardly miss a free lunch of his own.

There's a gloomy lesson there of course about the unlikelihood of any free lunch whatsoever, but that wasn't the one I had in mind. What I wanted to tell him was that the community of interest on which his fishing was based (shiners interested in plankton, snappers interested in shiners, boys interested in snappers) was as fabulous as anything else in the world. Wasn't he lucky, I would have told him, that the plankton had the brains to mastermind the whole operation —up to and including getting him to show up on this bridge at exactly the right time on the second Tuesday in September?

We've lost the ability to come at things that way. Or better said, we've lost the spunk to do it because we've been told it isn't intellectually respectable. Not that we haven't gained a lot from the discipline of trying to find out what the causes of things really are—from the scientific habit of leaving final causes pretty much alone and concentrating simply on what's actually happening. But in order to acquire that ability we've had to stand apart from nature. We've had to act as if nature could be properly understood only if we came up with understandings that have nothing to do with us—and more devastatingly, as if we ourselves, with our similes, our metaphors, our fabulous finalities and complicated poetic contraptions are no legitimate part of nature at all.

What that led to of course was the distrust of a good half of our equipment for looking at the world. In our fear of picking up an incorrect causal connection, we deprived ourselves of the freedom of rummaging playfully through all the connections we could think of. And that's a shame because it's precisely connectedness, interrelatedness, that's the most engaging thing about the world. We should be far more afraid than we are of the habit of assuming there's only one correct way of talking about it. To get a connection back-wards or wrong or to pick it up fabulously or poetically—to say the sun rises or the moon wanes, to think boats grow from seed or plankton have plans—is all small compared to missing the wonder of it altogether. Or as happens more usu-ally, to turning the world into an alien, tiresome place where only the least fabulous, least poetic—least human—reading of causality can be the right one.

Naturally I'm tempted (I'm as much a child of scientism as anybody) to issue a demurrer here. I feel the obligation to insist I'm not advocating a return to the bad old days of the pathetic fallacy when nature had human attributes rammed down its throat. I want to vindicate my respectability by say-ing how aware I am that the best scientists—their rigorous anti-finalism notwithstanding—have a wide poetic streak in them. And above all I don't want to give the impression that just because I've made up my own mind in favor of heart-warming versions of causality, I consider mankind excused from facing the cold confusion of facts.

But as I sit here by the creek, I decide not to care about all that. The world has already lost too much of its humanity by nothing-but-ery and only-because-ism. The boat buds, there-fore, and the floating islands, and all the finalities yet to be imagined—the more fabulously the better—stand without apology. I've taken my reductionist bath, thank you; it's time to start worrying about the baby.

two

THE TIDE

As I see it, the baby that's in danger of drowning in the reductionist bathwater is our sense of participation in the world. However good it was for us to kick the habit of thinking of the macrocosm chiefly in terms of ourselves as the microcosm—however many advances we made by learning to distinguish, for example, between what we thought we saw the planets doing and what they might conceivably be doing on their own—we still lost as much as we gained. The old way of looking at the world may have been less accurate than ours but it made for a friendlier universe. Watch.

When the ancients went out on a starry night, they saw, in one sense, exactly what we do: pinpoints of light moving slowly through the sky. What they thought they saw however is something we've all but denied ourselves. For us, the heavenly bodies are just so many hot or cold clumps flying around in accordance with laws that are themselves no more than descriptions of how such clumps fly. Our ultimate understanding, therefore, for all its fruits in science and technology, is profoundly tautological—not to mention dull. The whole system is turned in upon itself—an extremely large can with a great many stones rattling around in it but with no apparent reason for either the can, the stones or the rattling. And certainly with no earthly explanation of why we, on this particular stone, should feel happy, wanted, or even safe.

Compared to that, what our forebears saw was an absolute

picnic. For them, the heavenly bodies—whatever they were: dominions, principalities, powers or even hot rocks—were moving by desire in response to the attractiveness of the Highest Good. The dance of celestial beings was evidence not of rattling but of romance—and of the very same romance that moved human beings as well. That may or may not have been true (though in fairness it must be said it has never been proved false) but there's no question it made the universe a nicer place.

For all that though, in this place—down here below the bridge out of the wind—I grow cold. Time to be up and on the road again.

The next stretch, in winter, is the worst of the whole run. It takes me around the southeast bight of the harbor where the wind has the added advantage over me of a five-mile fetch across the frozen width of Shelter Island Sound. It gnaws through all six layers of sweaters and jackets. At a chill factor of one degree per knot of wind—minus five more for my own speed into it—the best I can do is cross my arms over my chest and run head down. Head empty too. At 6 below, philosophy freezes solid.

The road curves inland behind a point of woods just past the bridge over the next creek—if you want to dignify what's hardly more than a paved-over culvert with the name. Still, without such bridges this island would be a good deal more of a run than it is. As the crow flies, it's not more than five miles across in any direction. But as the crow looks down, it's a different proposition: all the creeks, inlets, bays and harbors make it a kind of corvine Rorschach blot on a blue background. As the human foot falls therefore—at least as it might have fallen before there were bridges—my guess is that keeping to the shoreline every inch of the way a runner could easily top a hundred miles.

The creek I just passed, incidentally, is one of the best places to study the dining habits of snappers. Watching them one fall morning, I had a *satori*, or illumination. Shiners, for some reason known only to God and their fellow baitfish, prefer to swim against the current. Perhaps it's because, like human beings, they cherish the notion they're the masters of their fate and so resist being pushed anywhere. Perhaps— since in a strong tide they make very little headway—they just settle for staying put. Whatever the reason, the result is that when the snappers come to get them they're almost always facing the wrong way.

I thought about that. A line from A. E. Housman went through my mind: ". . . the Inachean daughter, loved of Zeus, whom the gods of old, *more provident than kind*, endowed. . . ." In those terms, what had we here? Was nature more provident to snappers than kind to bait? Or was she kind to snappers and in the process provident to bait of an end made gentler by its coming unobserved? In any event, the heart of the operation was an *improvisa mors*, a death stealing up softly from behind. Lord now lettest thou thy servants depart at lunch, according to thy word. For mine eyes have *not* seen . . .

But it isn't only death that comes from behind. The whole of the future approaches from the same direction. We like to think that we walk into it forwards—that tomorrow is somewhere up ahead of us and that, while it may be hidden by mists, we're still at least looking the right way. But in fact the only thing before our mind's eye now is yesterday. It's the past we see clearly; the future we can't see at all. And we miss it not because of thick clouds or bad vision but because it's 180 degrees out of sight. What will happen *after this* is, quite literally, *aft of us*. We walk into the future backwards.

Crossing these same bridges at the same time every day therefore, I play a game with the tides. It took me a while to get it sraight even to myself but let me see if I can explain it to you simply.

Obviously, if you look down from a bridge on a given day and see the water flowing in, you know that if you wait there a few hours longer there will be high tide—or, should you see it flowing out, low. In other words, the tide appears to be facing frontwards, advancing in the direction of the goal it's already set for itself, moving knowingly toward a known future. To reach high water, it quite reasonably rises; to reach low, it falls.

However. If instead of waiting on the bridge that same day you return at the same hour the next day, you will find something surprising. Let's say that on Wednesday the tide was running out, that is, falling. Let's also say that it stood precisely at the halfway mark on the abutment. Finally let's give it credit for knowing its proper tidal business: let's agree that as far as the Wednesday in question was concerned, it was operating on the sensible theory that by ebbing it would fall lower yet—in other words, that it had decided on its future and was responding appropriately.

So far so good. But the question now arises: which future are we talking about? If it's the short one that will arrive three hours later on Wednesday, the tide can congratulate itself on getting the operation right. But if it's the longer future, the one that's scheduled for this same time on Thursday morning . . . ah, there's a catch to that. Because if you come by here then and look at the same falling tide flowing under the same bridge, the water will be not lower on the abutment but higher. The tide's more distant future, just like the shiners', came while it was doing something else—and was a quite opposite future to what it had in mind.

Hence my game. If, for example, I arrive on the bridge at seven and note that the current is flowing out, I face myself in that direction. Then I listen and try to hear, behind my back and the tide's, the voice that calls for not less but more water this time tomorrow. I haven't heard it yet exactly. But I know it's there. The system never fails.

One note. If, like the boy who was fishing off the bridge, you're tempted to say my system works not because of a voice that calls to the water but only because tides take twenty-five rather than twenty-four hours to make two full cycles, think again. Watch the reductionist "only" in there. I didn't postulate a cause for the phenomenon on which my game is based; I merely suggested a reason. True, my reason may be as fictitious as my boat buds. But—and this is the important, grossly neglected point—you cannot prove it so simply by specifying, even correctly, a possible cause.

Let me illustrate by sending the subject as far upstairs as possible. If I want to say it is the voice of God that summons the ebbing tide to stand an hour higher on each succeeding day—to gain, as it were, on the clock—you cannot refute me by insisting it's the moon that does it instead. That's like saying it's the mechanism of the piano and not Vladimir Horowitz that plays the *Emperor* Concerto. If God wants to summon the tides by giving the moon a periodicity that doesn't quite gibe with the earth's diurnal rotation, who's to say he can't? Maybe, as I admitted, he doesn't call them. But if he does, a lunar discrepancy is a perfectly reputable way of doing it.

In any case, don't be too quick to reduce the meaning of everything to nothing but a single cause. The world is full of dualities and it uses a lovely economy in bringing them off. Fall turns leaves yellow, and poets on, by one device: xanthophyll. Young love and nervous indigestion use the same set of bodily symptoms. If God speaks audible words, the sound waves in the air will not be different from those produced by us. If he wants to talk to you, it's no skin off his nose to use somebody else's voice. And if he desires to endow the world with significance, he's perfectly within his rights to settle, should he choose to, for a version of it that happens to be to my liking. There's a risk of course that

all that may be false. Remember, though: the only thing reductionism insures you against is seeing it even if it's true.
   With a policy like that, it's safer to be at risk.

three

THE CALL

I run the rest of my course in order if not in style: on the lope as far as the golf course, at ease by the third hole, at a walk for the time it takes me to recite some morning devotions in Latin, and back up to speed till I reach my front lawn and lie down to do the only two yoga positions I know: shoulder stand and plow. After that I split wood for the stove and, having thus cracked the door to futurity, finally decline from my solemn high drifting to the ordinary, half-understood purposiveness that makes up the bulk of the day. I shower, say Mass, have coffee with my best friend, work, cook, eat and at last sleep—back once again to the drifting that is the paradigm of it all.

I'm serious about that. Even the earth's course around the sun intimates it: the year interposes still seasons between the moving ones. When you wake and sleep as I generally do not by the clock but by the light, it's spring and fall—especially the beginnings of them at the equinoxes—that seem all action and change. Nature is on the go, and as the light races in or out you can't help but pick up speed in empathy. But at the solstices—in high summer or the dead of winter—change becomes imperceptible. The air's temperature, the day's light, the night's darkness, are in a rut for more than a month. It's only winter though that drives the stillness home. Summer has a thousand projects to keep the mind in motion;

winter, if it weren't for the woodstove, would hardly have one.

January especially. Purpose dies when the Christmas tree comes down; the rest of the month is pure drift. If there's a voice that calls—and above all if there's a call that governs— now is the time to hear it.

I think, first, of all my futures to this day. Like the tide's, they were resolutely double: short, plausible ones to which I propelled myself by intelligible devices, and long, mysterious ones to which I was drawn by a voice, half-heard and mostly misunderstood, from behind my back. Or by a death from the same direction. I became a priest to do the usual priestly things but I do only a handful of them now. I taught for two decades but haven't seen the inside of a classroom for years. I married and ended in remarriage. I wrote, and write still, but for how long I have no idea: if the voice is depending on publishers' advances to draw me, I could very well end up in the catering business.

That's not as grim as it sounds. True enough, at the moments the mystery barged in and elbowed plausibility out of the way—at the times when I was bounced off the bus of my predilections and stood clutching my battered bags, surrounded by entirely strange smells and noises—it wasn't all tea and cake. But that was only how the future felt, not what it was. After enough transfers, breakdowns, evictions and even willful refusals to stay aboard, you develop, if not a satisfaction with the way the bus line is run, at least an astonishment that it runs as well as it does. You always land somewhere. If you can remember not to waste your time wishing you were somewhere else, it's amazing what can happen.

And quite apart from moral considerations, by the way. People who talk about the future—particularly people who give God credit for being the managing director of the bus company—often make a mistake. In expounding the way they think the operation works, they feel obliged to exclude

certain dubious destinations from the company's general
guarantee. If you as a passenger get off at an approved future, they allow you coverage. So too if you are deposited,
through no fault of your own, at even unapproved ones: if the
bus crashes and leaves you in a ditch or if your fellow passen-
gers knock you senseless and throw you out the rear window
—if, in other words, you happen to land ethically at any of
life's less seemly stopoffs, at loneliness, disability, poverty or
grief—why, that's no problem. They will gladly certify you as
having arrived at a company-approved somewhere.

But if you depart catastrophically of your own accord at
high speed or, worse yet, contrive to leave safely when and
as you please—if, in short, you *sin* your way to your next
stop—they will insist the company has no further responsi-
bility for you. You are nowhere and nobody. Don't call them.
And above all, don't you dare think they ever called you.

As I said, that's a mistake. If there's a company worth
postulating at all, it had better be one that can put its call
through to any future, not just seemly ones. I think of Caia-
phas the high priest, finagling to get Jesus crucified because
it was expedient "that one man should die for the people and
the whole nation perish not." The future he had in mind was
only one more round of the game of political footsie on which
he'd built his career. Small matter. Whatever he thought, he
was tending willy-nilly to a future beyond all that: "this spake
he not of himself: but being high priest that year, he prophe-
sied that Jesus should die for that nation; and not for that
nation only but that also he should gather together in one the
children of God that were scattered abroad." The company,
you see, never loses a customer.

Not even Judas. Not even you or me. By hook or by crook
it gets us all to the ultimate somewhere: the resurrection of
the dead. The worst that can happen, at that irreversible
point, is that anybody who seriously thinks he'd like to be
somewhere else will be told, politely but firmly, to go to

hell. He has finally arrived at the single future of all futures. Pretending there's anyplace else to be is a game he can play if he wants to; but in fact he's got nowhere to go. Literally. And only. And always. Even lost, he's still at home.

You think that's a fast shuffle? Why, I've hardly even riffled the deck. If you feel uneasy at the thought of all those undesirables milling around in hordes at the eternal picnic ground—if you want to remind me how strait the gate and narrow the way is and how few there be that find it—just watch what a real shuffle can do.

Try to put together in your mind all the images we've used so far; the tides, the fish, the voice from behind everything's back serenading it inexorably into the future—even your own image of the strait and narrow. Then form a picture. Imagine a crowd in a courtyard. At one end is an archway broad enough for the Radio City Rockettes to go through shoulder to shoulder, high-kicking their way to hell and gone; at the other, a narrow embrasure high up in the wall. Everybody who even half looks for a way out finds the arch; hardly anybody discovers the embrasure.

Now then. What do you think that says about heaven? That it's empty? That the supper of the Lamb is such an exclusive affair it wouldn't even fill the upstairs room at Lutece? Think again. Think about, "I, if I be lifted up from the earth, will draw *all* unto me."

I know. You're going to tell me that's forcing things. But why shouldn't they be forced? Nobody reads scripture without making decisions. If it's all somehow true and yet seems in two places to contradict itself, you simply have to make up your mind which passage is going to get the harmonizing arm put on it. When I look at these texts therefore, it seems to me that it's the image of a crowd dividing itself into few and many that has to be soft-pedaled in favor of a Christ on the cross who claims he gets them all.

Put the images together under those conditions then, and

you have the full picture: *there's a vacuum in the embrasure*. All the suction of the universe is howling up the narrow way; all the power of the Word who mightily and sweetly draws everything to himself is roaring through the strait gate. Since everybody is facing the other way—toward the broad archway, toward futures that can be understood—the future that overrides them all takes everybody from behind. But even if someone fights it and escapes through the wide gate, it will still get him when he turns the first corner outside the wall. The only choice is to arrive at the ultimate future sooner or later. And all anyone has to do to arrive sooner is stop fighting and go with the flow. The universe reaches home for the simple reason there's no place else to go. Even hell is possible only in the house of many mansions.

That, I admit, *is* a fast shuffle. But then, what else could you expect? We're talking about a house nobody can beat.

four

THE LIGHT

I do apologize however for my precipitate siccing of the eschatological dog on you—for letting the subjects of resurrection, judgment, hell and heaven come at you all paws and yapping so early in this walk through the seasons. Unfortunately, it's the nature of the beast. We hold the ultimate future on such a long lead it sometimes meets us coming before we ourselves have properly got going. I shall try at least to shorten the leash.

Back to death. I owe you a good deal more than I've given on the subject. Not just because it's the prerequisite for all the other last things—course 101 in the eschatological curriculum, as it were—nor simply on account of its being the one empirically verifiable thing; but mostly because I'm talking about winter here. Between the dark and the cold, there's a whole term's lessons to be learned.

If, that is, we can manage to pay attention. For while we may think the connection between winter and death is obvious, and while it certainly was plain enough to previous ages, it's not quite that clear to a generation of chronic non-participants like ourselves. We're more cut off from nature than we think. In the ordinary course of our lives we neither share its rhythms nor have any feeling for its sequences. Mostly, our relationship to it is that of either consumers or victims: the former if it happens to strike our fancy, the latter if it doesn't. Whichever the case, though, nature itself gets hardly more attention from us than any other throwaway product.

Some items. (I am only recently, if at all, reformed—or to use the language of AA, I am not a recovered but just a recovering consumer/victim of nature: I illustrate from my own experience.)

Item one: morning. My first instinct when I want to find out the exact hour of sunrise is to look it up in the *New York Times* rather than at the horizon. Reason? The horizon's record of the event calls for my personal attendance upon it; *The Times'* does not. Result? From the *Times*, I get just the time; from looking out the window, I might have gotten illumination.

Item: morning, again. The question arises: will these dismal skies clear? The answer is available of course from either Ma Nature or Ma Bell; but except in the past few years, I always turned first to 976–1616. Result? Possibly accurate information (though not dependably so: this island is out on the edge of almost everything, weather included), but hardly a scrap of understanding. And certainly no sense of being in on a secret. How much nicer it is to be able to leak, all on my own, the details of nature's pending meteorological legislation:

> *Whereas* last night's wind was from the south and this morning's is from the southwest; and
> *Whereas* a wind shifting toward the west is a *veering,* and thus a *clearing* wind:
> *Therefore be it resolved* that, AT&T's representations to the contrary notwithstanding, a high pressure system, complete with attitude-improvement capability, shall be in place before sundown.

Item: noon. Problem: since I will be unable to place a necessary call to my editor after 3:00 P.M. today, and since everyone in the publishing business lunches till then at least, it is clear that I should phone by 12:00 M. But lacking a functioning alarm clock, how shall I remember to break from my writing in time? The possible solutions, b.p.c. (before participative consciousness) are as follows: set an oven timer every hour from 9:00 A.M. on (risking thus the almost certain omission of the crucial 11:00 A.M. reset); ask housemates to call me (inviting (1) their disgruntlement at me for complicating their lives and (2) mine at them for forgetting); listen for the 12:00 M. whistle (and not hear it because for the first time all morning I am in the middle of a sentence that hasn't fought me every inch of the way). Barring all those therefore, the best solution is the one that comes a.p.c.: make a point of remembering how a due north–south line would lie on my writing table; when the shadows of the window mullions fall parallel to it they will warn me of the approach of liquid lunchtime in bookland. Time to call.

Item: night. When shall I go to bed? I spare you the wrong answers (after "M*A*S*H," after "Love Boat," after Carson, after the hour of the Ronco salesman) and give you only the right one: when it's dark, unless for grave cause prevented— and then only upon guarantee of good company or good whisky, whichever shall first occur.

This last, I admit, is not necessarily a dependable example of either participation or consciousness, but let it pass. Enough about paying attention. Back to the connection we're paying attention to.

Between the victims of winter who hibernate in Florida and the consumers of it who spend their time trying to take the perfect powder in Vermont, the rest of us have precious little encouragement to do anything reflective either with the season or with the fact of death it so plainly bespeaks. Instead, we abolish as much of winter as we can afford to with oil heat and electric light and then have the nerve to wonder why, when death starts calling up our class, it can't similarly be bought off. Having denied ourselves our yearly sacramental reception of mortality, we have no choice, when it finally insists on showing up face-to-face, but to pretend it's something else. Hence the all-American funeral: three grains of sand and some vapid poetry directed at a coffin hanging vaguely in midair—the non-burial of the not-really-departed —a fate, if anything, worse than the death it tries to obliviate.

Back all the way then to winter. For those who either cannot or will not hide their eyes, its first and plainest casualty is the light. Above the arctic circle, of course, the demise of daytime is absolute; but over much of the globe it's still dramatic enough to have unmistakable effects: deepening cold and lengthening night. Of the two though, it's the darkness that's the governing consideration.

The world lives by light. I learned that twice: once in school by rote; and once as a gardener by experience. Where I live, the second crop of lettuces has to be planted by mid-August at the latest. If you dally as I did one year till the Labor Day weekend, you get next to nothing no matter how warm the fall. There simply aren't enough hours of sun.

The birds too bear that out. Cold weather, even though it's an effect of the shortened days, is not the cause nature relies on to trigger the migratory instinct. Stray warm fronts can linger on until no margin of safety is left. Witness the winter of '80–'81 here: it was so warm the vines were budding right up to December 24th; on Christmas morning it was one degree below zero. But the ospreys and egrets had all pulled out long since. How did they manage such brilliant scheduling? By the waning light that's invariably and infallibly noticeable—if not by smart human beings with artificial illumination and daylight-saving games, then at least by dumb animals who haven't talked themselves into missing the obvious.

Speaking of which, here's another fact—one it took me almost fifty years to notice. At the winter solstice when the light's dying produces the shortest day of the year, the light's death is not over. It lingers on at dawn for weeks as if to engrave itself on the mind. You no doubt gather, correctly, that I'm a morning person. And if you yourself are by contrast a confirmed slugabed, you probably also assume that I join you and the rest of the world's owls in rejoicing just before Christmas at the *natalia solis invicti*, the rebirth of the invincible sun. But I don't. No lark can. For the simple if strange reason that at the time of the day I most long to see a birth, the sun goes right on dying before my eyes. While the daylight does indeed begin to lengthen after December 22nd, the gain is all in the evening: the sun continues to rise later every day until well into January. You dance at sunset and think of spring; I sit *shiva* in the morning for three and a half weeks.

Or to shift to the imagery of the other half of the Judaeo-Christian tradition, I reflect on the dark truth that rebirth comes not after death but in it. I may believe that the light's resurrection is in the works; but in fact I experience only a continuing, deepening deadness. Like Martha standing with Jesus outside her brother Lazarus' tomb, I accept the generality of the light's return; but on these mornings, when this sun sleeps on in the tomb, I find it hard to believe that any command to come forth will work on something that dead.

Still, though, eventually it does come forth, morning as well as evening. But then no sooner has the light washed its hands of death than the weather takes over the job of rubbing our noses in it. The worst of the cold—*pace* the unreliable and overrated January thaw—is still to come. That's another oddity. Perfectly understandable in one sense (the reborn light is too weak to undo the ravages of its six-month dalliance with darkness); but perfectly exasperating in another (why give us hope and then drag us through three more months of what we hoped against). Nature, it seems, is less our mother than our wife. Quicker to forgive than to forget, she accompanies every absolution with a generous portion of pure hell just to keep us honest.

Winter, accordingly, does its wifely work: it hints at resurrection, but in a way that never lets us separate it from death. If that strikes you as odd—if you are in the habit of associating resurrection only with spring, if you think of winter as somehow incompatible with rebirth—let me show you something. Come outside for a walk around the property and a look at one of the January themes most people miss: the resurrection of trees.

There's an unreasonable prejudice against trees in winter. We're so used to picturing them to ourselves in full leaf that we shrink from their nakedness. I did that too—until I discovered the fallacy hidden in that imagery. For if you think of trees and resurrection in those terms you come up with a lame comparison.

Let's say, for example, that you want to draw a parallel between trees in winter and human beings in death. The first thing you're tempted to do, if you make the mistake of thinking of a tree as naked in winter, is to turn its springtime resurrection into nothing more than the resumption of a suit of leafy clothes. And if you then go a second step and try to tie that to human resurrection, you come up with some strange and unappealing propositions. You are not disposed of course to say that when we rise we simply put on gowns or tuxedos; but you are mightily tempted to say that, like the trees, we have two parts: one that dies as leaves die, namely, our body; and one that lives on as the trunk and branches do, namely, our soul.

For all I know, you may think that's a perfectly dandy analogy. I don't however. For one thing, leaves and bodies are not clothing; they're integral parts of their respective beings. For another, the whole of the tree goes into winter's death, not just the leaves. They may do the dramatic thing and drop off poignantly, but the tree itself does the potentially more dangerous thing: it stops the flow of sap—it comes perilously close to being not a live tree but dead wood. But, for a final thing, even in that death—even long before it, back at the end of the growing season—all the buds and therefore all the tree's new leaves are already in place.

Consequently, when I put all those facts together I come up with a different analogy. The tree in winter is no mere unclothed body; it's the skeleton of its former self. It has lost not its sports jacket but its life. I find that comparison appealing for two reasons. The first is that I have always loved trees in death—even permanently dead ones. They have an essential, not an accidental beauty; they sing clearly of what they're really about: line, structure, thrust, detail. Any idiot who can draw a lollipop can make a passable rendering of a tree in leaf: only an artist who pays strict attention to the anatomical wonder in front of him can do justice to a bare one.

But the second reason goes deeper. The whole tree goes into death, not just its leaves; and the whole tree rises—indeed with its new leaves written minuscule in tight buds, it's already risen now, even in its death. Its resurrection therefore is not the investiture of an imperishable soul with some more suitable body; it is the raising up—not only after death but in, with and through death—of what the tree really was all along.

Even as your resurrection and mine. The word has gotten about, unfortunately, that the gospel of resurrection is somehow dependent on the notion of an immortal soul. God, by that report, simply salts away the spirits of the departed (which incidentally would have dragged on forever anyway, salted or not) until he's ready to insert them into new bodies. The whole message is that the good news is simply an announcement that there never was any really bad news—that because the central, ultimate, finer me couldn't possibly have perished, my resurrection is merely the issuance of a niftier wardrobe which, but for some inexplicable oversight on the part of God, I probably should have been provided with in the first place.

But that's malarkey, not gospel. God makes the world out of nothing, not out of vaporous, pre-existent glop; and he raises it up out of death, not out of some spiritual half-life that's less interesting than a good collection of bones. And as the nothing out of which he calls us into being is always there to make us laugh at the incongruity of existence, so the death out of which we rise is perpetually present for the same reason. Like the trees with next year's leaves in their pockets, we too are in on the joke that applies not just to bank presidents, bishops and bureaucrats but all across the boardroom of creation: *while there's death, there's hope*. Mere continuance is a bore; and a rebirth that can't happen till after we're dead is a discontinuity. But the continuous resurrection of the continually dead . . . that's hilariously good news.

five

THE GARDEN

Before we end this tour of the grounds, come around to the back of the house with me. Even in winter I can't resist showing off the garden.

Until I came here I never had much luck growing things. Not even zucchini: the one time I actually succeeded in getting a few plants to come up, they produced only male flowers. I figured the world already had all the sexual vagaries it needed without my adding celibate squashes to the list, so I gave up on gardening altogether.

As it worked out though, I discovered I don't have a poison thumb after all—just the usual anatomical peculiarities of the backyard farmer: an easily sprung sacroiliac and a gluteus maximus that spends the month of May reminding me of its existence. This garden started out as a fifteen-by-twenty-foot plot but by plowing under more lawn every year I've now got what you're looking at: two hundred and twenty feet of four-foot-wide beds, all double-dug to a depth of two feet. If it weren't so cold I'd make you take off your shoes. The place you're standing on is holy ground.

Consecrated by me. At the price of uncounted quarts of perspiration and ten highly personal pounds. If you're not impressed it only proves you've never hand-turned forty-seven cubic yards of terminal moraine and then shoveled half of it through a screen to get the rocks out. Some of the stones on that pile over there weigh a hundred pounds—and there wasn't even a pebble among them that didn't object strenuously to having its twenty-five-century snooze in the ground interrupted.

STONE: What *is* that idiot doing with a spading fork?

PEBBLE: Beats me. You think he wants to move us?

STONE: Don't even mention moving. The last time the subject came up I was in Connecticut. There I was, minding my own business, when these operators come along and ask me if I'd consider getting involved in helping them build some dump called Long Island. Naturally, I refuse. Look, I tell them. For the first time since the volcano I'm part of a piece of honest-to-God continental real estate with at least a little potential for appreciation. I should risk my property value on a cockamamie island that doesn't even exist yet?

PEBBLE: How come you're here then?

STONE: They had this big, cold-hearted enforcer—Glacier, I think his name was. The best I could do was go along.

PEBBLE: You think this guy with the fork is Glacier again?

STONE: Nah. Glacier promised he wouldn't be back for thirty thousand years at least. This clown has got to be an imposter. I'm staying put.

PEBBLE: What if he insists though?

STONE: Listen. It's in my contract: thirty thousand years minimum rest. He tries to move me, I'll break his back.

PEBBLE: That's easy for you to say. But what about me?

STONE: You could get in his shoe. We can't take this lying down.

As it turned out of course, everybody took it lying down—

the gardener included, especially on Sunday nights. Still, the place puts out vegetables like a farm stand now. I'll try not to regale you with too much gardening talk, or cook's talk either. Let's just say that every summer we eat like . . . well, human beings (kings should be so lucky); and every fall we manage to fill one freezer and I don't know how many feet of shelves with the surplus. That part *is* fun. At least in winter when the reality of it is all in the larder and the labor only in the mind.

But as you can see there isn't much out here now: some rye cover on two of the beds and the rest of them left empty. Except, that is, for the end one I never did get around to cleaning up. It had some kale in it so I absolved myself from tearing out the other things till I'd had my annual winter feast of kale and *pinkelwurst*. A lovely dish. To paraphrase Oscar Wilde: it's the indestructible (kale withstands hard frost—in fact it's improved by it) accompanied by the inconceivable (*pinkel* is oats, fat and spices stuffed into a piece of intestine). Greasy greens.

I do see one thing though that I can give you for a souvenir. The cayenne pepper plants over there next to the kale are finished for good now, but a couple of pods that I missed are still hanging on. Here. Take a few. Freeze-dried, more or less, by nature herself. But be careful. Even dead, they're fierce. Some people have to wear gloves when they cut them up. Fortunately I don't, but I still have two dictates of prudence I learned the hard way. The first is, use a spoon and not your fingers to scrape out the seeds and membranes: hot pepper oil under the fingernails runs the burning bamboo torture a close second. The other is, if you've handled hot peppers during the day, don't rub your face when you go to bed at night. No matter how often you've washed in between, there'll still be enough residual oil on your hands to give your eyes a rude awakening.

Eating them of course is something else: Montezuma's revenge probably caught up even with Montezuma. Still, if you're a pepper lover you just put up patiently with the aggressive afterlife of chilies, thankful at least that it too eventually ends—that God gave them only an intimation of immortality and not the genuine article.

As a matter of fact, out here in the back garden it occurs to me to be thankful that he gave really immortal souls to nothing, not even us. Peppers may seem to have a ghost that doesn't give up and the trees in front of the house may hint vaguely at some kind of deathlessness—and lots of people have thought they had souls that went on no matter what— but back here where there's nothing but the bare bones of last summer's annuals, the real truth comes through: every individual thing in the world dies, returns in the end to the nothing out of which it sprang. Peppers may contain seeds for next year's plants but *this* pod and *that* plant on which it grew have simply had it—body, soul and all. And so in due time will everything else: from the individual trees on the lawn to the individual me to the one and only universe itself.

As I said, making human beings the single exception to that cosmic truth—concocting a spurious immortality of the soul to insure their survival after death—seems to me both unappealing and unnecessary. Unappealing because whatever life an immortal soul has after departing the body is at best a half-life after a half-death; and unnecessary because God, without any philosophical help from us, has already promised us a whole life after a whole death. Apparently as far as he is concerned death is no more an alien to eternal life than it is to natural life. In eternity as in time, death turns out to be the very engine by which the created order is run. What therefore do we gain by philosophically unhooking ourselves from it? To be sure, no healthy individual—vegetable, animal or human—goes around preferring death to life; but on the other hand why make a problem out of something that on every level has "solution" written all over it?

Take it from the top. Jesus obviously spoke well of death. At the price of being almost totally misunderstood, he made his own dying the touchstone of his messiahship. Admittedly he also emphasized his rising; but he kept the topics in order: death first, resurrection after that. And since he was a Jew, he most likely meant real, stone-cold death, not some kind of lukewarm half-expiration that would leave him with a Greek soul to vacation in while his body spent an unhebraically temporary three days in the tomb.

In fact, while we're on the subject of Jesus it seems to me he says pretty clearly that he considers our death to be the major contribution any of us makes to the plan of salvation. God apparently doesn't need our physical or moral cooperation any more than he needs our philosophical help. What he does count on is our death. That's the one thing necessary for resurrection. And since resurrection is the name of the game, it's the only thing necessary at all. I'd even be willing to say that for all practical purposes Jesus is our death and our death is Jesus. The statement could be cleaned up theologically by saying that our death is a sacrament, a real presence of Jesus—but that's just to keep the fussbudgets happy. The fact remains there isn't a human death anywhere in the world where the creating and reconciling Word of God isn't at work. Our death, in other words, passes the duck test: it walks like Jesus, it quacks like Jesus; therefore it is Jesus.

I find that a comfort. It means you can read "death" in all the places where he calls himself by other names and breathe easier as a result. For instance, when he says he is the Door of the sheep, you don't have to worry about whether you've got the right directions to find your way in: just keep going any way you like and by running smack into death's door you'll run smack into him. Or when he says the kingdom of heaven is like a treasure hid in a field, you don't have to sit down and calculate whether you've got enough money in the bank to cover the purchase price. The field is your death: by great good luck, it's the one farm nobody ever fails to buy.

Maybe you see now why I'm so chary of the immortality of the soul. It's a doctrine that goes out of its way to take a free, easygoing, let-God-do-it salvation and turn it into a book-keeper's nightmare. The gospel of the resurrection of the dead is good news precisely because it's catholic: it says that the only ticket anybody needs is the one ticket everybody has, namely, death. The immortality of the soul, if it's allowed to be the governing notion with which we grapple with the subject, tends mightily to flush all that down the drain. It leaves us, vis-à-vis the kingdom of God, exactly where we've been all along in the kingdoms of this world: stuck in line without a ticket. Worse yet, it guarantees us an eternity in which to fail to see the show. To be sure, the notion has been with us so long there's probably no way of junking it altogether. For my money though, we should at least take a vow to lock it in the closet every other week or so, and try seriously to face death without it.

Because the beauty of a world run by death is that it's merciful. There's absolution in it; things finally are over; the books we couldn't balance are simply closed. And the horror of a world full of immortal souls is that it's a nag that never ends. In its most logical extension, it becomes an inescapable circle of reincarnations lived through in the unlikely hope that some day we'll get it right. No wonder nirvana begins to look good.

I guess what I'm saying is that if unvarnished death doesn't seem all that bad out here in the backyard and if the philosophical denial of it doesn't seem all that helpful anywhere—and if Jesus, for good measure, told me it was all I needed to go home free—well then what's immortality going to do for me that'd be an improvement on that?

Repeat after me then: "When we're dead, we're dead." There. Not only is that a realistic proposition; it could make us feel positively like members of the club again.

six

THE EGG

What we need at this point of course are some fresh images of life and death. Having discarded the comforting if vague picture of a ghost that survives the shipwreck of the body, we're in danger of simply denying the possibility of eternal life altogether. Unless, that is, we can come up with another way of figuring it.

Think therefore of my life from birth to death. And take with utter seriousness the assertion that it's the only life I have. Don't be any more tempted to wonder what my life will be like in the year 2183 than you were to fuss over its details in the year 1783. In terms of time and space—in the world of when and where in which my threescore plus or minus occurred—my life just wasn't here at either of those times. Don't try to solve the problem of how I can have an eternal life by imagining pre- or post-existences for me. Let my life after I die be exactly what it was before I was born: non-existent.

Focus your attention instead on the days in between when I unquestionably did live; and then imagine that single, shortish life as held in two very different grips: mine on the one hand and God's on the other. Let me help by picturing them for you.

I have on my writing desk at this moment a hard-boiled egg that I intend to snack on by and by: let that represent the whole time of my life. Now since the first of the grips on my life is my own, I shall represent that by putting the the egg in my left hand and closing my fist around it: behold, my times are in *my* hand. But since the other grip on my life is God's—or more precisely, the grip of Jesus who as the Eternal Word of God makes and reconciles me at every moment —let me represent that by making a second fist over my left hand with my right. Behold again: not only my times but even my very holding of them are totally in *his* hand as well. The illustration is going swimmingly. We have even touched base with Psalm 31:15: "my times are in thy hand."

Examine next, however, the differences between those two grips. As I hold my life, I have only a weak and partial purchase on it. Any one of a thousand accidents can snatch it from me in an instant. And even if nothing goes wrong, I can hold onto only the smallest portion of it at any given moment: of all my times, only the present is really in my grasp. The past I hold only in remembrance—mental, physical or psychological; and the future I hold even less adequately—in guesswork, hope or fear.

Worse yet, I hold none of those times fully. As far as my present is concerned, I have an effective grip only on what I'm actually paying attention to at the moment. The pencil in my hand is under control; the bread I forgot I was making is now a hopelessly over-risen mess in the kitchen. And as far as past and future are concerned, things are worse still. Even if my memory of the past is better than it was of my bread there is no way I can go back to remedy a single mistake or improve a single performance—or even make sure I have not remembered the whole of it partially, tendentiously or wrong. And as far as the future is concerned, there is simply no way of getting to it at all. Except of course by waiting. But that does no good because by definition the future as such never arrives. When it does turn up, it's only one more present: what is really yet to be just hides out there in the dark as before.

In other words, not only is my grip on my times weak and partial, it is also unreconciled and unreconcilable. Change the illustration slightly: imagine the hard-boiled egg that represents my life as a peeled, sliced one. And while you're at it make it extremely large so that it can have as many slices as I have days—but leave all the slices together as a whole egg. Now then. As I go through the egg of my days slice by slice—beginning with my birth at the big end, proceeding delightedly through the days of youth and yolk and coming at last to the ever-decreasing slices of nothing but white—I can have a real influence only on the slice I happen to have reached and on the portion of it I have managed to pay attention to. If I wasted or abused a previous slice I can do nothing to help that now; any yolk I didn't eat today remains uneaten forever.

In God's grip however—as he holds the slices of my time —all my days, past or future, are simply present. To me they may be then and then but to him they are all now. The yesterday I cannot reach is as accessible to him as my present pencil is to me. The future I can only guess at is as known to him as any other slice of the whole egg he holds in his ever-lasting now. God, in other words, is the eternal contemporary of every moment of my times. Accordingly, there is no moment of them that is ever lost to him—and consequently no single, briefest scrap of my life that is not *as he holds it* safely ensconced in eternity.

Eternal life therefore is not another life after this one but simply this life as held eternally by Jesus—by the Wisdom of God who mightily and sweetly orders all things, even the things we disordered. And death? Well, for openers death is just one of the boundaries delimiting the things that make up a particular life. But it's a good deal more than that, and if you now put all the images together you'll see how.

Bring the peeled, sliced egg down to size again and put it back in my left fist inside my right fist. Then ask: what happens when I die? Well, obviously I lose my grip on the egg: my left hand, if you will, becomes ... nothing. All its records of its dealing with the egg, all its knowledge of details, all its mistakes, all its missed opportunities simply cease to exist when it does. When I'm dead, I'm dead: I have no brain to think with, no nose to smell with, no eyes to see with—nothing at all good, bad or indifferent with which to hold onto a single thing.

But when my grip goes, God's grip does not. The egg about which the left hand could do so little even while it had it, is still held for endless exploration in the right hand. All the days I could not keep are stored for me at home in him. My death therefore is not simply an end; it is an absolution. It is my release from my own radically imperfect way of holding my life and my introduction at last to the best of all possible ways of holding it in the hand of Jesus.

Do you see what we have done? By getting rid of the unnecessary philosophical baggage of the immortality of the soul we have in one easy leap gotten back onto the solid ground of the promises of the gospel. *Jesus came to raise the dead:* not to diddle those who were half-immortal anyway into some other slightly improved life but to take those who had completely lost their grip and give them back every last one of the days that he, as their resurrection and their life, had always held for them. He never met a corpse that didn't sit right up then and there because, although it may have been dead as a doornail on its own terms, it was alive willy-nilly in him and just couldn't help showing it.

When Jesus came to raise Lazarus, the dead man's sister Martha had her doubts. Like the rest of us she could imagine eternal life only as something out there—as a blessing to be achieved only after the protracted clanking of some religious or philosophical contraption. And therefore when Jesus told her her brother would rise again, the furthest thing from her mind was that it would happen on the spot: "I know," she said; "he'll make it at the last day." But what Jesus in effect said to her was: "Wrong! He's made it *now*. I am the resurrection and the life. He who believes in me, even though he's dead, will still live. And whoever lives and believes in me can't possibly die in eternity—because *in eternity* is exactly where I've got him for good." Lazarus, in short, might lose his own grip on his life but he could never shake loose of Jesus'. *Ergo* forth he comes when the Word who holds him speaks his name.

One more refinement of the illustration and we're through. If you want to do justice to the note of believing that Jesus insisted on with Martha, put a glove on the left fist. Do you see now? The life of faith is simply the constant willingness to trust that just beyond that glove there's another hand that holds our life along with us. We are invited to believe not that we *will* rise or that we *will* have eternal life, but that we have it right now and that we can enjoy it at the price of nothing more than slipping off the glove of unbelief that's the only thing separating us from it.

To me, that's a big improvement in the imagery department. With the old immortal soul I always ended up with a picture of myself sitting around the eternal body shop while God took his time about putting me on the lift. This new way I see a much more promising sign on the premises:

FATHER, SON AND HOLY GHOST
THREE MECHANICS
NO WAITING

SPRING

—

JUDGMENT

seven

THE FIX

I know. You are ready to cry, "enough!": enough winter, enough death—enough especially of this charley-horsing of the long arm of imagery. Take us to spring. And take us there straight.

I understand. My only justification is that my treatment, whatever else it may be, is at least a fair representation of winter: even a modest dose of it makes you wish it were over. I too am tired of the itch of these theological long johns.

Unfortunately, however, it is rarely my way to proceed anywhere by a straight course. My chosen method of exposition is a bit like wandering down an old-fashioned Main Street full of stores. One can of course do one side first and then the other (in the present case, for example, browse lightly through the four seasons before crossing over to more serious shopping in the four last things); but I prefer to criss-cross the street (some no doubt would say jaywalk) and work both sides of it by turns. I am happiest of all though when I can manage to arrive at the next logical step on one side by having the idea of it occur to me on the other. If you will scratch with me for just a little longer then, I promise to get you from death to spring in good order.

Follow out the imagery we've been using and see what it says about the second of the four last things: judgment. In the old way of figuring the day of judgment there just had to be an aura of bad news about it. Precisely because people refused to take seriously Jesus' suggestion that at death we lose our souls as well as our bodies, they pictured themselves before him at the last day as fully loaded with the baggage of their former misdeeds. In spite of his having said "He who finds his soul will lose it [the Greek word is *psychē* and means "soul" or "life" interchangeably] and he who loses his soul for my sake will find it" (Matt. 10:39) they endowed themselves with the unending inconvenience of an unlosable soul. Then quite naturally they scared themselves half to hell at the thought of having to stand in front of a judge with guilt unerasably written all over them.

Their mistake obviously lay in imagining that on their day in court there would be some vestige of their former selves that could properly be chewed out for their crimes. They may have believed that Jesus would give them new and glorified bodies at the resurrection, but inside those bodies they envisioned the same old inglorious soul waiting like an eternal sitting duck to be condemned to the firing squad. And they got themselves to that unenviable position by failing to take seriously yet another of the more startling passages of scripture: chapter 2, verses 12–14 of Saint Paul's Letter to the Colossians. "You are buried with him in baptism, in which you were also raised with him through faith in the working of God who raised him from the dead. And you who were dead in your trespasses and in the uncircumcision of your flesh, God made alive together with him, having forgiven us all our trespasses—having blotted out the handwriting of ordinances that was against us, setting it aside, nailing it to the cross."

The first thing to note about that passage is how nicely it jibes with the notion that my eternal life is simply my present life as Jesus holds it in his resurrecting right hand. Saint Paul tells the Colossians not that they *will be* raised by

Christ, but that their resurrection is already a fact in him and that their baptism is a sign of it right now. (You might also note how ill it consists with the old image of an immortal soul tapping a non-existent foot while it waits for a resurrection . . . but enough, finally, of that point.)

The second thing to be observed about Saint Paul's language is how completely it fits the new imagery of judgment we're working on here. We've said that since we utterly lose our own grip on our lives at death, all that's left of them after death is what's in Christ's grip. But if that's true it means that no one comes to the judgment with his times in his own hand. Everyone who is drawn to Christ, now or ever, comes with his grip on his own life broken, eliminated, absolved by death. And that means quite astonishingly that Christ judges us as *he* holds us, not as we hold ourselves. And finally therefore—since he holds us already reconciled—it means that in some deep and almost hilarious sense, the last judgment is in fact rigged in our favor.

The image lurking in this passage accordingly is that of a divine fix being in even before the court is called to order. If I may, let me try to flush it for you.

Item. God seems to give himself the runaround on the subject of judgment, particularly in the Gospel according to John. To begin with, the Father—for whose ultimate gratification the whole business of creation and reconciliation is undertaken—*judges no man:* he has, Jesus insists, committed all judgment to the Son.

Item. The Son, however, to whom the nasty job has been assigned, waffles mightily on the subject. "What, *me* judge? I don't judge anybody. I came not to judge the world but to save the world."

Item. Nevertheless, when he does finally shoulder his judicial robes, he continues the mystification by playing fast and loose with the responsibilities of his office. First, as Saint Paul says to the Colossians, he takes the handwriting that was against us and blots it out. Pity the poor prosecuting attorney! He approaches the bench to request a reading of the charges and all the judge does is rummage idly through his papers. "My, my. It was here a while ago but I don't seem to have it now. Oh well; case dismissed for lack of evidence."

Item. Not only that, but if the prosecution tries to rebuild its case by a fresh investigation of our crimes, it is out of luck again. All our misdoings have been nailed to the cross—lost to history, sequestered in the darkness of Jesus' death and passion—so that in the resurrection there isn't a one to be found.

And one final item just so you don't feel too sorry for the prosecutor who has to hunt for the truth in the midst of this festival of irreversible judicial error. Do you know who he is? He is the Paraclete, the *paraklētos*, the Advocate, the Heavenly Attorney himself: God the Holy Spirit, of one mind and substance with the Father and the Son. What we have therefore is a top-to-bottom conspiracy to obstruct justice. Not only can't the D.A. find the evidence against us, he's so in cahoots with the judge's plan to acquit that he isn't even seriously interested in looking for it. Sent by the judge, instructed by the judge, he argues for nothing but what has already been determined by the judge, namely, that there must be therefore now no condemnation. He helps not the cause of justice but the infirmities of our otherwise hopeless case. He makes his intercession not for the system we have offended but simply and exclusively for us—and with all the courtroom antics he has mastered in an eternity of unutterable groanings and other theatricalities.

If that doesn't say the fix is in, I don't know what does. It takes the image of a God out to get even with us and stands it on its head. Or, to be accurate, it takes the old, upsidedown notion of a vindictive God and sets it back on its *vindicative* feet again. Because given the whole thrust of what

God was up to in Jesus—given, that is, the flat assertion that he was out to save, not to condemn the world—the only possible picture of Christ as judge is one that shows him not as the retaliator of our crimes but as the vindicator of our lives as he now holds them reconciled in himself.

"Look," he says, opening his right hand to his Father and at the same time to the totally surprised you and me who didn't even know we existed, "This is what I had in mind. Pretty nifty, huh? Why don't we all have a beer and call it a day?"

I could, of course, go right along in this side of the street and pick up some heaven ("Gee thanks, Jesus, I never knew I could look so good"); or some hell ("Listen, when I want somebody to do me over, I'll ask—meanwhile, why don't you just stuff it?"). But a promise is a promise so I won't.

Anyway, I just hit on the perfect reason for crossing back over to spring.

eight

THE HEDGE

I admit that giving the Eternal Word a last line like "Why don't we all have a beer?" comes perilously close to making Jesus sound as if he's announcing Miller Time. I'd apologize, but as it works out it's precisely his calling it a day that takes us straight to spring. (Besides, I deserve credit: at least I resisted the temptation to draw parallels between "let it be Löwenbräu" and "let there be light.")

In any case, when Jesus does call the judgment a day, he gives it a quite specific name, the *last* day. Take John 6:39, for example: "this is the will of him who sent me, that I should lose nothing of all that he has given me but rather raise it up at the *last* day." Or John 12:47 (where, incidentally, he also intimates what I've been saying about judgment as vindication, namely, that it's his forgiving, saving word on the cross that's the last word on our condition): "I did not come that I might judge the world but that I might save the world. He who rejects me and does not receive my sayings already has what judges him: the word that I have spoken, that's what will judge him in the *last* day."

But in calling it "last" he obviously doesn't mean it's a day that has nothing to follow it. Rather he's saying that it's the point in history at which—just as in the beer commercials— the old order finally gives way and the new order it was always headed for *at last* begins. All of which is caught best not in the original (where the Greek word *eschatos* has the same way-out-at-the-end flavor as the English *last*) but in the Latin version of Jesus' words: the last day is *dies novissimus*, the *newest* day, the *freshest* day—or to take the delightful twist it acquires when it's turned into German, it's *der jüngste Tag*, the *youngest* day. Behold therefore the transition I promised you: if the judgment is indeed the youngest, freshest day of the world, we can learn more about it from springtime than from anything else.

Run with me again. It's the last Saturday of April and we're on our way to our usual resting place at the north end of the golf course. But this time with some differences. For one thing it's a pleasant, flat calm 57 degrees. For another we're shortcutting the top loop of the run with a detour through an orchard. And for a last, even though it's before 5:00 A.M. and we've been running for half an hour, the sun is not yet up. By a combination of God's marvelous disposing and man's loony proposing, today's sunrise (around 5:07) will be the earliest of the year. If we don't dally too long we may even hit high ground soon enough to catch it breaking over the bay. Hit or miss though it'll be our last chance till next April: after tonight's daylight-saving games, tomorrow's sun will sleep till 6:05. Even on June 21st we won't be able to wake it earlier than 5:31.

Nevertheless since we've got the drop on it today, let's take our time. More was left here for our inspection than just an orchard.

One of the pleasures of running, at least in the distracted way I go about it, is exploration. I don't think people actually experience much of that nowadays. Whenever they go some-place they haven't been before, they're almost always in a car. That's hardly exploring though. Routes you can cover in a car have a certain sameness about them. Oh, I know. You're going to tell me there are a thousand different kinds of roads. Well of course there are—for a while at least, until the shopping malls grow together and cut off the scenery completely. But there are a billion different kinds of roads if you're not stuck behind a wheel.

The biggest thing wrong with gas-powered exploration is the nature of the automobile itself. Its ability to make remote places accessible invariably tricks you into thinking there are no enchantments except at some distance from home. Which is a mistake because the real joy of exploring lies not in the negative satisfaction of finding someplace you never saw before but in the positive thrill of discovering that a place you always thought you knew has inner chambers you never even suspected. Hidden passageways and tucked-away rooms—inscapes rather than landscapes—are the very stuff of exploration. But you find them only on foot. No one ever caught an inscape from a car.

And even on foot you can miss them. Getting the boy out of the car is one thing; getting the car out of the boy is something else. For the first few years I ran, I still acted more as if I were driving than on foot. In fact I literally drove myself; I clocked distances, checked times and bragged about mileage. Worse yet, when I ran by a pretty girl my first reaction was not to turn my head but to look up into a non-existent rearview mirror for a second glance. Fortunately I only put up with that kind of nonsense for a while: my neck fairly quickly regained its 180 degree capability. It took me a bit longer to learn simply not to drive myself at all.

As a matter of fact I ran around the outside of this place for months before I finally stopped assuming there were just houses in here and actually went and looked at it. Come on. Follow me in and see some of the benefits of deprogramming yourself.

What we're headed for is a pretty-much-abandoned twenty acres or so of meadow, orchard and woods that lie in the center of what has to be the most microscopic municipality in the state of New York: the incorporated village of Dering Harbor. The village's other distinction, by the way, is

that it may also be the least poverty-stricken such entity: the
waves that lap against the docks of its twenty-odd private
residences produce some of the world's most expensive
sounds outside Saint-Jean-Cap-Ferrat. It wasn't always so exclusive though. At the turn of the century it had a big resort
hotel complete with chapel, steamer landing and carriage
house: city dwellers, hundreds of them at a clip, used to
come here for a combination of sea breezes and devotional
uplift. The day of religious R and R is long since gone of
course and so are most of the facilities that provided it: fire
got the hotel, storms took care of the landing, and somebody
carted the chapel off and made an art gallery out of it. Only
the carriage house is left but it sort of makes up for the rest
by providing us with the first of the inscapes. Behold! The
genuine article: horse-ramps up to the doors at both ends;
brown shingles not too badly weathered; and a roof-beam
that doesn't sag nearly as much as it might considering its
length.

How long would I say it was? Well the building has a
dozen windows on a side; so if you allow something like ten
feet per stall at each window and twenty for the carriage
rooms at the ends, you get a hundred sixty feet. What's in it?
Well, mostly not horse and carriage junk. I don't know who
owns it but somebody's got a pretty decent sailboat stored in
the south end. There's also a mysterious stack of short tile
pipes against the west wall on the outside. I have no idea
who put them there either, but I do know they make nice
holders for wooden spoons. Got one in my kitchen in fact.

What's on the other side? The orchard; come and see. It's
not in bloom yet and it's been untended for so long it doesn't
even flower much, let alone bear fruit. Still, it's a great place
to walk through morning by morning, especially in the spring
when the angle of the light on the trees is different every day
and green shoots begin to break through the mat of dead
grass. In summer, though, you stay clear of it: too many

ticks. This island is one of the places (along with Nantucket and Martha's Vineyard) where you can pick up a social-climbing malady called babesiosis: after giving you a usually unnoticed bite, the almost equally unnoticeable deer tick surprises you with a blood parasite that produces nausea, fever, anemia and jaundice. One bout is enough.

At the edge of the orchard though, just beyond the line of copper beeches and weeping beeches over there, is a better surprise: a greenhouse. Not just a run-of-the-mill commercial job either: this one is a genuine, old-fashioned richman's-plaything. Actually it was a rich woman's plaything, or so I've been told, but in any case it's complete with two wings (glass porticoes, no less, at either end and curved glass all along the eaves) plus the obligatory Greek-revival center section with porch and a big, fenced-in garden out in front. There! Is that a toy and a half, or isn't it? Once again, I'm not clear who owns it now but whoever does isn't around much. Somebody seems to put in a little time on it—there are plants inside that look quite good—but the care doesn't extend to the garden. That's been allowed to go luxuriously to seed. Come June it'll be fence-to-fence lupine in more colors and combinations than you've ever seen.

Wild! That's the reaction I finally have to this place. Not just because it's gone more than halfway back to nature but because even the original cultivation seems to have been done by a mind not given to taming its enthusiasms. The size of the orchard, the pretensions of the greenhouse and the profusion of lupine all argue a certain penchant for excess. But to me what clinches the case is the apparent wildness over beech trees that possessed the mind of the lady who laid out these grounds. Not content with weeping beeches predictably and hugely sad or with copper beeches merely and expectably magnificent, the monomania drove its victim to something I for one have never seen anywhere: a beech hedge all along the wooded northeast side of the property.

Yes, I said hedge: over a quarter of a mile of it. Made years ago by planting beech saplings two feet apart and then trimming them into a wall as they grew together. Except at twenty-foot intervals where larger beeches were cut into balls to break up the monotony.

When I first came here it was kept trimmed to perfection —so much so that before I actually explored behind it I assumed it was the first line of defense of a mansion to end all mansions. But as you've seen, it isn't. It's just a bizarre frame around an ambitious boondoggle—cared for, the story goes, by the original gardener even after the original owner had passed on to the ultimate beech grove in the sky. And cared for out of love, I like to imagine—perhaps not just for beech trees but even for the late lady of the manor herself. Is there any truth to that? I have no idea. Islands, having tenuous ties with reality, tend to breed romance. Still, I do know that about three years ago somebody stopped trimming it, so maybe there's something to it after all—if not here then hereafter, with the two of them on the eschatological plantation singing "O Mother Dear Jerusalem":

But there they live in such delight,
Such pleasure and such play,
As that to them a thousand years
Doth seem as yesterday.

The tune, by the way, is "Materna," more commonly set to the words of "O Beautiful for Spacious Skies." Pick it up in the middle with me; it fits my conceit about this place to perfection.

Thy vineyards and thy orchards are
Most beautiful and fair,
Full furnished with trees and fruit
Most wonderful and rare.

Thy gardens and thy gallant walks
Continually are green;
There grow such sweet and pleasant flowers
As nowhere else are seen.

Quite through the streets with silver sound
The flood of life doth flow,
Upon whose banks on every side
The wood of life doth grow.

But even if I'm wrong to bark up the romantic tree, I know I'm right about the eschatological one. For here at this hedge, on this spring morning, nature delivers an authentic *last* word. I don't know how much attention you've ever paid to beech trees in bud but, for my money, they're the very paradigm of judgment. In March, the buds are still mostly what they've been all winter: pointed, tightly rolled little cigars with dark wrappers. But as April swells them, the outer scales lighten and the almost invisible hairs at their edges grow and brighten into silver gray. Finally however, as the buds open and the leaves disclose themselves, the authoritative word comes: like Jesus opening his right hand at the day of judgment and showing us creation as he holds it, the beech tree says, "Here: *this* is what I had in mind."

Spring is the youngest, freshest day of the world, the definitive disclosure of what life was meant to be and of the resurrection that won't take no for an answer. No matter that on this very hedge there still hang last year's leaves, dead and dry, the voice that calls forth this year's insists on a new creation: pleated and perfect, tender and pale, the leaves break out of the buds in soft green clusters—the closest thing in the world to the lips of God.

At the end of the Book of Revelation—at the last day of the old world when the first heaven and the first earth have passed away and the new Jerusalem comes down from God, prepared as a bride adorned for her husband—the Lamb who sits on the throne says, "Behold, I make all things new."

The Word's final word is nothing less than what he says springtime by springtime as he vindicates the shape of everything and everyone afresh. And our reaction to that word—unless we turn from it with deaf ears and estranged faces—cannot help but be the heart's astonishment we've always had at the world that springs fresh from the speaking of the Word.

We shall not cease from exploration
And the end of all our exploring
Will be to arrive where we started
And to know the place for the first time.

We simply love all youngest days. The last one can't possibly be an exception.

nine

THE CLOCK

A while ago, before I got going full tilt on inscapes and beech trees, I raised a passing eyebrow at the looniness of setting the clocks ahead an hour every spring. That wasn't enough. I feel the need to escalate my disparagement into a full-scale potshot. Springtime's flood of light is just as much a judgment—a youngest, freshest word about what nature has in mind—as is the bursting of buds. All we do by our day-light-saving pretensions is put fingers in our mind's ears. We so preoccupy ourselves with the fiction that we can tell the sun what part of the day to lighten that we miss the astonishing fact of its lighting upon us at all.

It's a case of the tough customer in us driving out the grateful legatee. Rather as if you were to make a will guaranteeing me a better dinner wine every night for six months and, just when the choice clarets began to arrive, I insisted I couldn't enjoy them unless they were served to me one chair away from my present seat. Silly. At least it would be if it weren't also mischievous. Daylight saving time is one of those inventions of modern society—like the cocktail hour, the income tax, the presidential primary and the expense account lunch—that is suspect in its origins, inequitable in its application and unsound in its philosophy. It is a king with no clothes on. To the barricades, then.

First, as to its suspect origins. Like all tyrants, it hides its lack of natural right to rule under a myth of divine birth. Ask school children. Daylight saving time, they will tell you, sprang fully formed like Venus from the brow of Benjamin Franklin. Pure buncombe of course; but another triumph of fiction over fact nevertheless. Franklin did indeed advance the idea—but in a piece of whimsy written a hundred and thirty-two years before the country lost enough of its sense of humor to take him seriously.

Historically its origin was demonic, not divine. Its adoption was first advocated by crass commercial types who reasoned that if you could con people into thinking the sun was shining an hour longer, you might well get another sixty minutes worth of haymaking out of them. And it was actually instituted in wartime—to increase the production of devices designed to stop people from making hay altogether. (For the record, the dates are: Germany, 1915; England, 1916; USA, 1917.)

My personal disenchantment with it however derives from the second of my charges, namely, that in practice it results in inequities. For one thing the daylight it purports to save is all in the evening. For another the dates at which it undertakes to begin and end this one-sided rescue operation (late April and October) serve only to skew things even worse. And for the last, rather than making the summer more bearable, it in fact obtrudes the sun's heat on the very part of the day that needs it least. Let me illustrate these points in order.

You know of course that I am a confirmed morning person. But suppose a bit further and make me also *per impossibile* a true believer in the notion that daylight can be saved by fiddling with clocks. Does that mean I must accept the present system quietly? It does not. Instead it immediately raises the question of why the savings are not deposited at the beginning of the day rather than at the end. Why not to the larks' account rather than to the owls'?

I am aware that owls do in fact run the world and that they

show little interest in whose ox is gored as long as it isn't theirs. But I am also aware that their principal argument for "saving" daylight in the evening is the fact that if we didn't do it the sun in solstice would rise at the, to them, monstrous hour of 4:31. Accordingly, since the best defense against such people is to be as offensive as they are, I propose a new system. Set the clocks back instead of forward in the spring and frighten them with an even bigger hobgoblin: sunrise at 3:31.

Note the excellences of this proposal. First it is quite natural in spite of the unearthly screams they raise at it. Somewhere to the north of here the summer sun already rises at that time (indeed, to the north of *there* it never even sets). What is truly monstrous is not the dawn's early light but the darkness of minds that presume to judge the whole of nature by what happens only south of New Haven.

More to the point though, a morning daylight-saving system would actually improve summer evenings. Think for a moment of what we call "the heat of the day": the hours, four in all, bracketing the sun's transit of the meridian. In reality of course no amount of clock changing can make a degree's difference in their oppressiveness; the best we can hope for is to put supper as far away from them as possible. But what in fact does the present system do? It drags the heat out till 3:00 P.M. so that no one wants even to look at food, let alone cook it, till 8:00 P.M. And what does that in turn do? It leads us to ply ourselves with cucumbers and gin in the effort to kill time—only to end up killing appetites and brain cells instead. No. Far better to set the clocks back. That way the heat will be off at 1:00 P.M. and we can dine at 6:00—hungry, cool and sober in the bargain.

But it is not only summer evenings that would benefit. Were my proposal to be left in force all year long (the French, who do nothing by halves, already have that arrangement as their present system) winter mornings would

be better too. At least for joggers. Obviously the early runner's greatest need as he slogs his way through the dark time
of the year is for light and heat. Since both however are
functions of how long the sun has been up, it would seem to
me that any sensible system of resetting clocks should be
designed to have it rise as early in the day as possible. But is
that the case now? Far from it. Consider. In winter solstice,
the sun rises at 7:18 or so standard time. Therefore to keep to
a starting hour of 6:00 (so I can be showered, clothed and in
my right mind to begin the day around 8:00) I would have to
run two miles in pitch darkness and the whole distance in
almost urelieved cold: break a leg, freeze to death, or both.
Putting the sunrise back to 6:18 would get me out in twilight
and back in sunlight—and with better odds on my survival.

On the other hand, if for some strange reason the authorities could not see their way clear to allowing me morning
daylight saving time all year long, I would at least petition
them to put the changing of the clocks at the equinoxes and
not, as they have it now, a month later. Consider once again.
Here at the end of April, sunrise occurs at about the same
time as it does in mid-August (both points being equidistant
from the solstice); by the same token however, at the end of
October it occurs when it does in February. To a morning
person that is not just asymmetry; it is cruel and unusual
punishment, especially in the weeks just before the autumn
change. The October sun rises so late it might as well be
Christmas. Seeing December once is quite sufficient. Nobody needs a preview.

But enough stones thrown. Mindless systems invite mindless implementation. Since my morning daylight saving time
would probably fare no better in the authorities' hands, I
take it back and retreat to higher ground.

I once had another *satori*—this one while struggling to
remember the eminently forgettable mnemonic: spring
ahead, fall back? spring back, fall forward? It suddenly

dawned on me that whichever it was, its meaning was the reverse of what it seemed. The maxim was not a piece of advice about which way to turn the clocks, rather it was a warning against any turning of them at all. Like "Spare the rod, spoil the child" it was one of those masterpieces of English syntax: a double imperative used to state a condition that implies a negative. "*If* you set the clocks ahead in the spring," it said in effect, "you will just have to put them back in the fall, so"—and this is the crucial point—"don't fiddle with timepieces at all."

I like that. We take clocks too seriously as it is; who needs to credit them with the ability to create or destroy even an hour? Only we have such power. The crucial periods of our lives—the high times, the due seasons, the decisive conjunctions in which time is really redeemed or killed, the youngest days on which the ultimate, defining words are spoken—are creatures of no clock. They come to us not because metal hands impose them but because we ourselves recognize them, hear them and seize them—because finally instead of waiting to be told what time it is, we dare, with such light as we have, to decide what it's time for.

I like that even better. Tonight, I think I'll leave one clock unchanged just so I don't forget.

ten

THE TIME

Speaking of clocks, I spent my first few years on this island trying not to look at them. After almost three decades of letting my life be dominated by a watch, I saw my rustication as a sign from heaven to stop putting myself and others on procrustean schedules. My old habit had been to cut short every appointment for fear of being late for the next; here on "the rock" where there hardly ever was a next, I resolved to make present company a permanent exception to such fidgets.

It was a salutary resolution. "He that believes shall not be in haste." "In returning and rest you shall be saved; in quietness and in confidence shall be your strength." Not to mention the fact that no matter how covertly you sneak the consultative peek at your watch, the quality of the attention paid to your supposed consultee flagrantly declines. Still, while I did manage to be less manifestly rude about time, I found it harder than I'd expected to disregard the subject altogether.

Especially in the mornings. Even after four years of rising by the light and refusing even to look at a clock before noon, I found that I still almost always knew what time it was. Nature, it turned out, had an even more inexorable schedule than man. She might vary the time of sunrise wildly from one solstice to the next but she did so in an order so predictable that I not only could but did set my mental watch by it: the change was slow and almost imperceptible at first; then faster and more obvious till the equinox; finally it retraced its way gradually back to no noticeable change at all. Willy-nilly, therefore, if I could see the sun come up, I knew the time practically to the minute. Like the traveler who had so mastered his itinerary that he knew it was Belgium because it was Tuesday, I would say to myself at sunrise, "Hmm, mid-April—must be damn near 5:25."

Not only that, but depending on where I was vis-à-vis the sun on any given morning I could be as time-ridden as ever. If I reached the harbor before it rose I was inordinately proud of myself; if I saw its light angling down the bedroom wall while I was dressing for my run I got profoundly depressed. Worse yet, even if nature cut off her time reports with cloudy skies, I went right on spooking myself with atrocity stories gathered from man. When you run the same roads all the time you get to know the schedule of every pickup truck and school bus on the route. If 8174-RFC passed me on the first leg, it practically ruined my day: I was already a half hour late.

To make a long story short therefore, my efforts not to know what time it was finally collapsed in the face of the world's seemingly unbreakable resolution to keep itself on schedule. I wasn't discouraged though. For one thing, I found a breach in creation's resolve: if you go running on a cloudy Sunday morning, not only is the sun's rising unnoticeable and its subsequent angle undeterminable; even old 8174-RFC is home sleeping off Saturday night. Neither nature, man nor God apparently gives a fig about time on such a Sabbath.

But for another, I learned something even about the times that nature wouldn't let me forget: I may equate them with some abstract set of parameters but she doesn't deliver them to me for that purpose. On this spring morning she cares most not whether I can say what time it is when the light wakes or what temperature reading it may produce but whether I can perceive, in the light that is the world's life, the word of judgment by which she proclaims what she has in mind. Once again, I'm being invited to find out what it's time for.

Unfortunately, since the invention of the incandescent lamp and the $99 fare to Florida, we've tended toward the belief that with few exceptions, it's always time for nearly everything—if not outdoors, then in; if not under this sun, then under another one farther south. Yet whenever people root themselves deeply in a single place on earth, none of that is true. No hour is simply *time:* it is *high time* for one thing and *not time* for another. And no season of the year is a mere collection of minutes: it is a *due season* whose arrival can be missed as well as met. The real earth, unlike the world of night baseball, winter football and endless summer, is a place where too early and too late still mean something, where discerning the times is a matter of life and death.

After all is said and done then, my fidgets were not entirely the product of bad habits. There is indeed a pressure of time on creation; but it is not the whimsical one of men and clocks. Rather it is the deep, insistent one flowing straight out of the heart of light: "Now!" it says. "It's *time.*" And nowhere is that urgency more manifest than in spring. Air warms, snows melt, sap rises, birds sing, animals rut, onion grass shoots up and even young persons' fancies—unless they carefully busy themselves with dark projects like removing sexism from the language—lightly turn to thoughts of . . . precisely what the light had in mind all along.

Why do I belabor something so obvious? Because it is not obvious at all, even to many of the best minds among us. Let me quote you a bit of egregious point missing from no less an authority than the author of the article "Seasons" in the *Encyclopaedia Britannica:*

. . . only the extreme seasons have a distinctive character; if the husbandman's round had not left so profound an impression on European speech, spring and
autumn would be considered merely transitional periods, hardly worthy of names coordinate in rank with
summer and winter.

Husbandman's round, indeed! Tell that to the raccoons!
Coordinate in rank, yet! Does he think Lady Spring pines
away because, by the standards of his strange beauty contest,
she has neither the twenty-two-inch waist of winter nor the
forty-four-inch bust of summer? Does he imagine she envies
them their bizarre temperature readings?

It is as silly to think of spring solely in terms of such sec-
ondary considerations as it is to think of the day of judgment
simply in terms of morality. Both are announcements not of
who has more or less of what but of a youngest day in which
the light wills that all should have life abundantly. And in
both, the invitation is not to compare the present with the
past and see if prizes are warranted but to accept the present
as a prize already given and to savor the freshness of the new
creation.

What's that you say? You rather thought the judgment *was*
about morality? Oh dear me, no. Why, it is as idle to consider judgment a moral category as to think that spring . . .
But then if you didn't see the analogy one way, you won't see
it the other, will you now? I think I shall come at the subject
from a different direction altogether.

For God did not send his Son into the world to judge
the world but that the world might be saved through
him. He who believes in him is not judged; he who
does not believe has been judged already because he
has not believed in the name of the only Son of God.
And this is the judgment, that the light has come into

the world and men loved darkness more than light because their deeds were evil. For every one who does
evil hates the light and does not come to the light lest
his deeds should be exposed; but he who does the truth
comes to the light in order that it may be clearly seen
that his deeds have been wrought in God. (John 3:17 ff.)

Let me gloss the text for you in order.

Not to judge but to save. What do these words do when
they are set against the imagery, scriptural and popular, of a
God who keeps stricter books than even the IRS? What do
they make of the tradition that depicts our last meeting with
him as an inexorable and probably catastrophic audit? They
make mincemeat out of it, that's what. God, by this text, is
not about to condemn us for our moral failings but to save us
in the very thick of them—even, indeed, *through* them. And
not, please note, by doing a cosmetic rewrite of our account
books so he won't have to look at the record of our pecula-
tions—let alone by waiting until we have made ourselves sol-
vent—but by pouring his own life's savings into our bankrupt
operation and by ruining himself in the process. *While we
were yet sinners, Christ died for the ungodly.* We are accepted not because we made ourselves acceptable but because God simply dropped dead to the whole subject of
acceptability.

He who believes in him is not judged. How can that be, do
you suppose? How can mere belief—not reform, not solven-
cy but the bare act of trusting someone else—spare us from
condemnation? I will tell you how: *he who believes* is not
judged because as a matter of the only fact there ultimately is
nobody at all is judged. How could anyone be when, on
God's own showing, his Son came only to save—and to save
not less than everybody at that: "I, if I be lifted up from the
earth will draw *all* unto me." The Lamb of God who takes
away the sins of the world nails every last one of them, not

just a particularly attractive selection, to his cross. Believing, you see, actually *does* nothing. It is not a transaction by which we cause some effect, by which something that was not the case is made so by appropriate action on our part. It is simply our willingness to trust that a work we never did know how to do—and that we couldn't have accomplished even if we did—has been done for us by a gracious other. Faith is not an act by which we enter into a deal that we're responsible for bringing to fruition; it's just saying, "Sure, why not?" to somebody who claims he can deal out all the fruits to begin with. And therefore faith is not a matter of more or less, not something to be judged by how confident we feel or by how much or little we know. It is a dumb and blind yes to someone about whom the only thing we can really be certain is his Name. "No man," Luther said, "can either know or feel he is saved; he can only believe it." Luckily though, he needs only to believe it, because if it's true at all, it's true already.

He who does not believe is judged already because he has not believed in the name of the only Son of God. How plain that is: condemnation comes not because of sin, evil, turpitude or failure; it comes because of unbelief. In chapter 20 of the Book of Revelation, Saint John the Divine says that in the last day he "saw the dead, small and great, stand before God; and the books were opened: and another book was opened, which is the book of life." God, it seems, has one shining purpose but two sets of books: the first set, "the books" that were opened; and the second, "the book of life." How do I distinguish those sets? Well, I take "the books" to mean the record of our wretchedness as we hold it in our own grip—that vast personal library of unreconcilable horrors whose catalogue contains more than enough to demand our condemnation forever. But I take "the book of life" to mean that same record as Jesus holds it reconciled in his resurrection—after our grip on it has been broken and absolved by our death. The record of my days, you see, is written in both sets of books; and though they are universes apart, both sets are true. But while all the evils I ever did, knew or felt may lie eternally in the first set, they cannot be found in the second. The book of life contains nothing but a new truth that sets me free—and since it's the only book the Son shows to the Father, that truth is mine simply for the believing.

At the last day therefore Christ judges only between belief and unbelief. Not between good and evil—because, by the vindicating power of his death, both of those are held reconciled in him; and not between those who have cooperated with grace and those who have not—because his grace is sovereign and reconciles all things without so much as a by-your-leave. He judges only between those who, in the face of his flat assertion that they have been saved and not judged, choose or do not choose to believe him. To be sure, it says later on in Revelation that "whosoever was not found in the book of life was cast into the lake of fire." But to me that has to be read *under* the rubric of "he who believes in him is not judged" rather than *against* it. If he did indeed come to save, then the only sense I can make out of "whosoever was not found written in the book of life" is: whatever fools there might be who, contrary to the assurance of the Word, refuse to believe they'll find their names there if they look. I realize that implies a certain eschatological sweetness on the part of God—and that a lot of people who prefer a world run by a Tough Customer will fault me for it. However since I personally have no confidence that I could last even five minutes with anyone but a Supreme Pussycat—and since it does say we should taste and see how gracious the Lord is—I find myself indisposed to getting that sweetness out of my mouth.

And this is the judgment, that light has come into the world . . . Which light? Why, the Light who by the very act of his coming lightens every man (John 1:9). Do you see the image? It is one in which all human beings who ever lived or will live stand bathed forever in an invincibly flattering light beamed at them by the Light himself—by the Word of God "from whose fulness we have all received, and grace upon grace." It is the picture of a world lit up by the favorable judgment of one who came only to save: "By my lights," he says, "you're okay. As I illustrate you for my Father, you too are the beloved Son in whom he is well pleased. That's true. Believe me."

. . . and men loved darkness more than light because their deeds were evil. Stay with the image. The Light shines on all; but some, refusing its flattery, turn their backs on it and stand looking into darkness of which they alone are the cause. Rather than behold their substance as he illuminates it for them and for his Father, they stare blindly at their own shadow. It is precisely the turning of their backs, therefore, and not their evil deeds, that condemns them. It is not darkness itself that drags them down but their *love* of it. The Light would make light of their evils, but they will have none of it.

For everyone who does evil hates the light and does not come to the light lest his deeds should be exposed. Of whom does the text speak? Of certain baddies who, as opposed to those of us who are goodies, happen to have done naughty things? Not at all: "everyone who does evil" is, quite simply, *everyone* period. "There is none good, no, not one;" the scripture has concluded—locked up—*everything* under sin, so that what was promised to faith in Jesus Christ might be given to those who believe. The human race, being totally devoid of good guys, hates the light without exception. Every man, woman and child Jack of us would rather not see the contrast between the messy drawing we have made of ourselves and the quite outlandish illustration Jesus insists is the only true rendering. And yet though all our deeds are evil and all of us fear the light, the Light is kindly and—if only we will love it more than darkness—will take away both our evil and our fear.

Therefore . . . *he who does the truth comes to the light*. . . . It is an odd phrase. Not "does the good" but "does the truth"; not "has avoided evil" but has admitted the simple fact of his love for dark shadows and allowed the light that cannot be overcome to shine them into oblivion.

. . . *in order that it may be clearly seen that his deeds have been wrought in God*. The last day is not an occasion on which God congratulates us upon certain deeds good enough to deserve the title "wrought in God"; rather it is his blessed assurance that all our deeds, even the worst, were done nowhere else but in the presence of the Light. It was not that we managed to get a few spendid performances enshrined in the eternal Hall of Fame but that we never did a single act that was outside it: in the true Light, we simply looked like winners all along.

In the last day therefore, we will discover not something we suddenly became but the very thing that, except for our unbelief, we always were. The day of judgment will not show us what he will do then but only make plain what he did when he chose us before the foundation of the world. He makes all things new not because he does something new at a certain point but because he has always willed newness. The circuitry by which our darkness is lightened has never not been plugged in; the deep, insistent pressure out of the heart of light has, in his perpetual spring, always been on. At the youngest day we shall simply see that fact and hear, for good and all, his oldest, freshest word: "Now! It's time!—for what I've always had in mind."

And just as that judgment is light years away from the category of bare moral bookkeeping, so springtime, with its light that renews the world, lies far beyond the measurements of any mere encyclopedist. Which, if I recall, is what I was trying to get at. In any case though, Q.E.D.; and goodnight, Lady Spring.

SUMMER

—————

HELL

eleven

THE SUN

I realize I may have made the next pair of items on the agenda seem a bit problematical. While summer still looks like a fairly straightforward subject, my rosy exposition of the last judgment as a triumph of sweetness and light has probably led a good many to wonder quite literally what in hell I've left myself to talk about.

The wonderers are divided of course in their reactions. Some—to my mind by far the more congenial sort—rejoice. They never have understood how a chronically guilty race could manage to work itself into enthusiasm for everlasting punishment and they stand ready to acclaim what they assume will be my irrefutable proof in two paragraphs or less that no such thing exists. Indeed the only worry in their kind hearts is whether I have not perhaps ruined the correspondences of this book by depriving myself of eternal miseries to set against the temporal torments of July.

Others, though, wonder more darkly. What have I done, they want to ask me, with the fire and brimstone they knew and loved? They have met my kind before: universalist nicenellys who run around letting convicted devils off scot-free, quack theological surgeons who remove God's backbone when he's not looking. You could not give us hell, they say, if your life depended on it. Go preach to jellyfish!

Unfortunately I must disappoint both groups—thrice each for that matter. A first time because, though they have different reasons for expecting me not to, I shall indeed give them hell; a second because the damn I give will undoubtedly please neither; and a third because I shall make both of them chew their nails awhile before giving it to them. If heaven can wait, so *a fortiori* can hell. However convenient I might find it to stay on the eschatological side of the avenue where the Eternal Stove Works is right next door to the Palace of Justice, it is not my way to make such plausible progress. Across the street we go then to summer—and for the moment with not a theological care in the world.

But not without care altogether. "Nothing too much," said the ancient Greeks; and ever since, wise men have called moderation the key to a happy life. Yet summer is immoderate in everything. It is too hot and too humid, too cloudy and too dry; it has too many of all the worst things: insects, mildew, head colds, jellyfish, pool parties, two-piece bathing suits, stretch marks, sunburn, jello salads, zucchini quiches, steaks à la charcoal lighter and cocktails *ad nauseam;* and it has too few of all the best: civilized meals, quiet evenings and early beds.

It is a measure of modern man's loss of discernment as to the good life that he equates summer with happiness. True, there is a skin of reason on the equation: it reminds us of being let out of school as children. But it is a thin skin: by the end of August, when summer has had its perfect, dreadful work, children are universally mad, sad and bad. That such a season, productive of no moderate anything whatsoever, should be seen as the *tempus opportunum* of human well-being . . . oh, well. Even God never said we were an easy race to save.

Perhaps though if we could find someone who understood the root of summer's excesses—someone by nature undeceived as to the speciousness of its charms who could alert our minds to the real source of its mischief—we might not be quite so bamboozled. Fortunately the search is over before it begins: having myself never once, man or boy, been seduced by summer's blandishments, I am the very person we want.

Consider a mere handful of my qualifications. Beginning at the age of three I was forced every summer to wear scratchy woolen bathing suits. Even if I sat perfectly still all day on the beach, they made chafe marks on my legs that looked like the aftermath of a bungled amputation. At the age of nine I suffered near-terminal herpes from too much sun on my nose—and from ten to sixteen I sported so much zinc ointment on it that I became known to my friends as The Beak. Finally, in ripeness and perfectness of age, I have not been to the beach these last four years; I am not now nor have I ever been an outdoor cook; and firmly convinced that the Ruler of the universe made trees immune to sunburn for good reason, I refuse on religious grounds to sit anywhere but under them—or under structures made from them—until the hour of sunset or the 21st of September, whichever shall first occur.

As you can see I have already put my finger on the nub of summer's excesses. There is no created good of which there cannot be too much—and therefore by a kind of physical Murphy's law, there is not a single such good of which there will not sooner or later be too much indeed. Only of God can we have not enough. With even the highest natural good of all—the light I have just so extravagantly praised—a bellyful is the easiest thing in the world to get.

But since so many people treat the summer sun with an irrational reverence, let me present a reasoned case against it. Mere horror stories cannot convert such souls. If they have not been deterred from their idolatry by factual tales of the sun's bizarre effects on the world outside them (squashes that turn into dirigibles overnight), neither will they be persuaded if I sensationalize such effects ("The Tomato Crop That Ate Shelter Island!"). Rather what is needed is an argu-

ment that will convince them of a threat to their *inner* world
—an *argumentum ad vanitatem,* as it were, that will enlist
their self interest (which may be the only interest they have
left) in the service of truth.

Accordingly, my principal charge against the light of summer is that unlike the illumination of antecedent and subsequent seasons—not to mention the light of the Light
Himself—it is unflattering. Who is there with so much as a
smitch of good sense about the effects of lighting on life's
intimate theatricalities who would consent to attempt even a
flirtation, let alone a seduction, under a ceiling fixture?
Merely fatigued tissues beneath the eyes strike the beholder
as nothing less than sagging pouches of marbles. An otherwise acceptable nose casts a shadow that looks like clown
makeup. Cheekbones, high, low or broad, look as if they
were rented for the occasion.

Quite plainly it is only lateral lighting—from a candle perhaps or a shaded table-lamp—that is gladsome light. And
when it comes to the sun, it's only in seasons other than
summer that it sidles thus kindly into our lives. Indoor
spaces, for example, delight us in winter. We may think that
is simply because they're warm, but the real reason is that
they're full of light—low, soft, old-gold southern light. Any
room that receives it romances us to the point of heartbreak.
To make love in a motel in July is only to make love, and in
a drably functional space at that; to lie there on a December
afternoon is to risk the winding of one's clock beyond repair.

And the same is true outdoors. "It was just a summer romance" is the case more often than we'd like, and the reason
why such boy-meets-girl dramas close so regularly out of
town is not the actors' unreliability but the lighting desig-
ner's incompetence.

The sun that shines in June at noon
Paints a landscape like the moon.

We may croon and spoon our hearts out till Labor Day, but the mercilessly downlit stage on which we do it mocks our efforts. Romance thrives on small perceptions and minuscule contrasts; the midday midsummer sun all but obliterates them. Twin lovers' shadows that in fall might have danced downhill before us are driven underfoot and out of sight. The light from common water and the grace from simple stone, so unfalteringly grasped by recollection in autumn, are struck from the mind's hands by the glare of summer. Every texture that might have compelled us with the color of its countries is bleached and hammered flush into forgettability.

No, the light that flatters rather than flattens—that leaves us green in memory rather than bone-white in oblivion—is not the light of summer. It's the autumn sun that etches us into each other's mind; "remember" rhymes only with months of sidelong light. My *argumentum ad vanitatem* therefore reaches its conclusion: since nobody's image can be enhanced by a season dedicated to putting everything in the most uninteresting light, no serious self will try to advance its interests till September. Or to couch it in terms of one of my master texts: "In heaven it is alwaies Autumne"; summer, by contrast, is just one hell of a time to be remembered in.

twelve

THE EVENING

That was of course extreme. But then if summer is indeed the seasonal analogue to hell, such excess should be expected. Permit me to continue my immoderate development of the correspondences.

Omitting further detailed proof of summer's ability to make me look and feel bad—passing over, that is, the effects of its heat (if I keep my clothes on, I look like an unmade bed; if I take them off, I look like an overstuffed chair) and of its humidity (I have long since ceased to be aroused, arousing or arousable upon a soggy August bed)—I proceed directly to my central criticism of the season. Summer's profoundest effects on human nature are substantial, not accidental, moral, not simply aesthetic: it makes us not only seem bad but actually be so. I shall construct my case from the ground up.

In the spring, I go gladly to my wintered-over garden. Small matter that all the beds have to be turned over by hand (not to mention by arm, shoulder, back and rump) to a depth of a foot and a half. No object that the device with which this is done (a two-foot-wide iron "fork" with seven eighteen-inch tines and a pair of handles six feet long) weighs some seventy pounds and handles about as easily as the portcullis of a medieval castle. A mere trifle that manure and compost must be carted, spread and forked in. A bagatelle that seed must be bought and planted. It is all nothing to the joy of watching young plants sprout in weedless, bugless beds—of being able to say, right along with nature herself, "This indeed is what I had in mind."

But by the second week in July my own intentions for this Eden have come a cropper and nature's have turned into a mystery. My neat, parochial husbandry has been subsumed by her untidily catholic agricultural management. For bell peppers, now read peppers, pigweed, purslane and dock; for eggplants, eggplant trunks neatly topped by Colorado potato beetles armed, apparently, with felling axes. The garden that hardly a month ago was a triumphant extension of my single-minded purpose is now a war zone where competing self-interests fight to the death. It has become not the world I intended where one benevolently right ego would prevail but a world of a hundred egos where every last one of them thinks it's righter than the rest.

It is that condition of rampant righteousness—of endemic violence perpetrated by a host of pretenders not one of whom will admit anyone else's claim—that is the very essence of summer. In spring, all of us try our best to think otherwise; but by deep July, when the sun shines equally on the just and the unjust, the gardener knows the truth: where everybody is convinced of his own rightness things are a mess. Heaven—on earth or otherwise—happens only when somebody is willing to give in; as soon as nobody can afford to lose, you get hell.

Except, as the gardener also knows, it doesn't quite work out that badly in the world of minerals, vegetables and dumb animals. For although the war that's hell goes on each summer as the remorseless kill-or-be-killed proposition it really is, each winter guarantees that not just somebody but nearly everybody will in fact give in. What comes so close to being hell in July and August has its fit of righteousness interrupted by November and December. This year's attempt at paradise may have led to nothing but thorns, thistles and sweat, but precisely because so many of the participants had the grace to drop dead, the encouragement to try again next year is overwhelming.

And even where there isn't seasonal death—in the tropics, for example, where summer reigns for good—there's still just plain mortality: the ant that eats the plant feeds the frog that eats the ant; the jungle floor is a paradise of compost. The universal self-interest that on its own principles should destroy the world simply doesn't: luckily, the selves wear out before their interests can finish the job. Where there's death, there's not only hope, there's ecology.

Until of course you get to the animals who though not dumb are stupid enough to make the self's rightness their chief interest in life. That's us, obviously: the race that can't let an argument die; the menaces who would destroy the world if they thought it would prove them correct; the idiots who can't conceive of composting a single one of their bright ideas even if all it does is sit around and stink. And the heat of summer is the time to see us in action.

It is evening. The August day has done its worst and is now trying, within the limits of a deeply flawed character, to make amends: a sudden shower has wet the concrete walk and a light breeze lifts the poignant fragrance to the nose; the light at long last comes indeed from the side; we stroll, glass of Gewürztraminer in hand, through that same cool of the day that led even the Lord God to take a walk in his garden. And what do we hear? Let me list the sources of sounds:

1. the lady across the street: even in winter, behind double-glass windows, she has a voice that can etch glassware in the next county; tonight we catch her in mid-disquisition on the subject of her teenager daughter's moral character: no mother in the world, we reflect, has quite her ability to scream extra syllables into the word "slut";

2. the boy next door riding a motorcycle around the house while his father, on a power mower, threatens to break very spoke in the bike's (*expletive deleted*) wheels unless he gets his (*obscenity*) off it and helps rake the lawn;

3. the man in back discussing with his wife not only the dinner party for which they are presently dressing but also all the other parties they have attended in the last decade: he is being warned not to drink, or else; she, not to invite certain gentlemen—a number of names are bandied about: we catch Hairy Harry, Bobby-Baby and (*scatological remark*) Smith—to put their hands all over her; she observes that at least that would be somebody's hands; he, that if she wasn't continually threatening his manhood . . . but we are out of interest even before we are out of earshot, so we finally turn our attention to

4. the children of the neighborhood: silent all day, they have now at 7:45 p.m. begun a game that thanks to the nation's gutless capitulation to the evil of daylight saving time will go on till nearly 9:00; the gist of the game is threefold: first, a child who is "it" does, or fails to do, something whose nature remains permanently obscure; second, despite this lack of clarity, at least seven of the players spend not less than ten minutes in a vocabulary exercise the purpose of which is to find as many words as possible to describe the first child's general lack of truthfulness: finally, in spite of the fact that this activity is carried out at a volume of seventy decibels and at a pitch never lower than high c, a continuous obbligato an octave higher and twice as loud is provided—apparently by the device of applying lit cigarettes to the bare feet of all the children under five.

In the end though, darkness and a kind of peace descend.

As we come up the garden path, the one audible trace of all this noise is the plaintive sound of weeping and gnashing of teeth. The wrongs so wrathfully perceived have gone west with the light and only the sad perceiving of the perception remains.

And that is very close indeed to hell. Not quite the state itself of course, but that's only because the wine of the wrath of man is usually served cut—if not with the milk of human kindness at least with the water of human distractibility. It may make us drunk, disorderly and hung over; but as long as it's diluted with sweet reason or forgetful feelings, it does us no permanent harm.

But if it is distilled—if we run our perceptions of right and wrong through enough fiery retorts, if we boil away in the alembic of our minds all the facts, all the extenuations, all the wrongs themselves, everything but a pure intuition of utter rightness—we have the very liquor of damnation, the 200 proof *eau de mort* that not only blinds the drinker for good but lays low everyone in his path. For the neat spirit of hell is a championing of the right so profound that it produces a permanent unwillingness to forgive, an eternal conviction that wrong should be prevented whenever possible and punished whenever not, but this it must never under any circumstances be absolved.

And while that unhappy state of mind may take a bit of achieving in this rough-and-ready world where feelings fade and rightness becomes a bore—where the woman screaming "slut" and the children shouting "liar" mercifully and commonly run out of steam—it is nevertheless as possible a state here as it is an allegedly certain one hereafter. You recognize it: the two sisters who have not spoken in years and who, though they can hardly recall the outrage that divided them, have kept the perception of their respective rightnesses about it at full boil; the betrayed lover who denies the beloved and ends the affair rather than forgive the betrayal and live happily ever after with both. It's the old story of The Righteousness That Ate The World.

And its effect on both those in the right and those in the wrong is always disastrous: the right, it condemns to a perpetual resistance of wrongs that resistance is powerless to remove; the wrong, to a certainty that they will not be pardoned, ever. For both, mere emotions that might have passed have become angelic principalities that can't die, forget or absolve. They have come at last to that state where unforgiving bastards are totally and eternally in charge of everything: Abandon Hope All Ye That Enter Here.

That's the hell of hell. That's why it's presided over by the rightest angel who ever lived. That's why it's the least human place in the universe. And that's why, though earth can sometimes indeed be heaven, it can never quite manage to be pure hell: there is always the chance that out of pure feeblemindedness if nothing else we might just drop the subject of being right.

We ask that God's will may be done "as in heaven so on earth," and we follow that by praying to be forgiven only as we forgive. The link we establish between earth and heaven, you see, is a human link and the virtue we attach most immediately to his will is a human virtue: mercy top to bottom, here as there; pardon all around, there as here. Heaven is not the home of the good but of forgiven forgivers; hell contains only unpardoned unpardoners. Neither place, of course, is inhabited by anything but unpardonable types: it's just that everybody in heaven, God himself included, has decided to die to the question of who's wrong; whereas nobody in hell can even shut up about who's right. Hell is where the finally, unrepentantly righteous and the finally, impenitently wicked have literally forever to enjoy their final, unendable war.

Which brings us, finally, to the subject.

thirteen

THE PORCH

To be truthful though, it brings us only to the front porch of the subject. Or to be totally and embarrassingly frank with you, to a series of front porches.

One of the marks of a good theologian is the care he takes not to lead others into vexed subjects without adequate preparation. True, it's a trait that's produced not a few theological treatises that were mostly preface—all porch and no house, as it were—but it's a sound trait nevertheless. Accordingly, if I'm going to construct a doctrine of hell for you I should at least avoid the mistake of building one that opens directly onto the street. The subject is quite dreadful enough; to drag you straight into it off the sidewalk or, worse yet, to let its grim, unadorned facade uglify the whole neighborhood would be disastrous. Let me bring you to it one porch at a time.

The first of these anteplatforms is a low, simple one designed to make clear the limitations of theological language in general and of hell-talk in particular. It is characterized by a series of short planks:

Faith is trusting a person;
Theology is throwing words at things
    nobody really knows beans about:

Therefore theology can never be the kind of
  money-in-the-bank proposition
  that faith can.

Still, theology is probably inevitable;
And the things it throws words at *are*
  important:
So unless you forget it's just a word game,
  it's not a bad thing to do on
  rainy afternoons.

On the specific topic of hell therefore:
  If you remember that all
  you really grasp about it are the
  words you've been given to grasp it with;
And that the first rule of the
  game is not to lose any
  of the words;
And that the second is to extract
  only as much sense from each
  word as you can without emptying it
  of sense altogether;
And that the third is to be sure that the sense
  you extract makes the least nonsense out of
  all the other words;
And that fourth is to bear in mind that
  whether you manage to extract any sense from them
  or not, the reality they're about
  will, thank you very kindly, still go right on
  doing its own thing, whatever that may be:
Well then, you probably won't do
  too much damage and you
  might even have a little fun—
  provided you don't forget how
  you got this far to begin with,
  namely, by going back to START, that is:

Faith is trusting a person;
Theology is throwing words at things
    nobody really knows beans about;
And so on.

In any case, here is a fair sampling of the words by which
we're invited to grasp the subject of hell:

The outer darkness

The bottomless pit

The lake of fire burning with brimstone

The second death

Everlasting fire prepared for the devil and his angels

Everlasting punishment

Where the worm dieth not and the fire is not quenched

Where there is weeping and gnashing of teeth

It is a summery eschatological assortment indeed and it
has heated more than one theologian into a lather of immod-
eration. Yet if we remember the rules of this first porch there
will be no reason for excess. We will claim no *proper* knowledge of hell at all: not of its guest list, nor of its census fig-
ures, nor of its pastimes—and certainly not of its location,
duration or existence, nor even whether it has any such or
not. We will claim to know only the images contained in the
words of scripture and, without forcing them either out of
consideration or into a jejune literalism, we will try to give
them the fairest shake we can. On to the next porch.

The second platform leading up to the subject of hell is
constructed entirely of lumber taken from the doctrine of

judgment—and taken in particular from the notion of judgment as vindication rather than vindictiveness. There isn't a
board here that doesn't square with the idea that the judgment is the triumph of the sovereign, reconciling Word himself—with the image of the flattering Light who illustrates us
for his Father on the youngest, freshest day of the new creation.

For if we were to wander into the consideration of hell
from any other notion of judgment—or from none at all—we
would perforce see it as nothing but an arrangement by
which a God who gets his jollies from socking enemies
around assures himself of an endless supply of punching
bags. To those who delight in such a Deity, of course, this
porch will seem unnecessary, if not offensive. But for the rest
of us who dare to hope that his character may be just a tad
more promisingly paradoxical than all that, it is an indispen-
sible preparation.

Take note of what putting a reconciling judgment in front
of hell does. It insures to begin with that all the wretches
who end up inside the place will have been told, right out
here on the porch, that as far as God was concerned there
was no reason at all for them to go in and be wretched. "I've
got you all fixed up in Jesus," he will have said, "and if you
want to stay out here in the sunshine on the veranda, why I'd
like that just fine. Juleps all around, Peter, and don't spare
the bourbon."

Next, though, take note of your immediate theological
reaction to such an indiscriminately gracious offer on the part
of God: it makes you wonder how he manages to be so nice
without at the same time being divinely feebleminded—how
he can sit there with all the garbage that omniscience has
collected through all of time and still not be bothered by it.
And it makes you wonder especially how, in this fit of terminal niceness, he can distinguish between heaven and hell.
The same mindlessly congratulatory judgment having been

made the front porch to both, there seems to be no significant difference of clientele between them.

That, you see, is a genuine theological poser: the realities involved are completely beyond your ken, and all you've got to work with are words and images. Nevertheless, if you play the game carefully you can come close, if not to an understanding, at least to a clue.

Basically there are three ways of coming at the question: one Awful, one So-So and one Not Bad.

In the Awful one, you say that God, being omniscient, simply has to remember every last bit of rottenness forever. That's a loser not only becuase a heaven full of garbage is practically unthinkable but also because scripture says the exact opposite in so many words: "Their sins and their iniquities I will remember no more."

In the So-so way, you take that quotation more or less literally and say that God somehow forgets everybody's vices. That gives you a possible heaven of course; but for the vast majority of us whose lives consist of volumes of evil as compared to pages of good, it sounds as if only a drastically edited version of ourselves is going to make it to the eternal publication party.

Or, finally, in the way that's Not Bad (which is as close as a theologian ever gets to Best of All), you play it both ways and say that he somehow manages not to let his knowledge of them get him—or us—down.

Of those three, only the last two are worth incorporating into this second porch—and only the last can bear much weight at all. Nevertheless, since we seem to have gotten ourselves irrevocably into the theological construction business, let me fit them in for you as quickly as I can.

The question immediately raised by the literal way of solving the problem of how God deals with his knowledge of evil is quite simple: how can he forget if he's omniscient? And the answer of course is: he can't—or at least we can't say he does without making mincemeat out of the English tongue. God is God and there's no use answering a minor theological question in a way that knocks the major topic out of the subject altogether.

All is not lost though. In the gospel scheme of things, God also took on humanity in Jesus: "the Word was made flesh and dwelt among us." Christians hold that in the incarnate Lord, divine nature and human nature are united unconfusedly but inseparably in one Person. God has provided himself therefore—in the Person of the One whose name is both Son of God and son of Mary, both Light of Light and Jesus of Nazareth—with access to all the possibilities of both natures. As divine, for example, he cannot die, but as human he can. As God he is almighty, but as man he can't press more than about 250 pounds.

Follow that up however: as God he can't forget, but as man he can. Ah! Is that the lead we're looking for? Shall we hold that when we say God remembers not our sins, what we really mean is that he employs the notorious forgetfulness of the human mind for the job? Shall we postulate that as Jesus failed to remember, say, that his disciples were out rowing all night in a storm or that his mother wore a size 7AA shoe, so God in Christ consigns our sins to the same short memory?

I think not. The inevitably whimsical obliviousness of a living human mind does not seem to me a safe repository for information that's supposed to stay dead forever. For though our failures to remember are frequent, they're anything but permanent. With a little help from the emotions or the senses, all kinds of things, good and bad, come back to us. The nose remembers without even knowing it remembers:

one breath of a perfume not smelled for years and we are, astonishingly, back at our high school prom. And feelings hold grudges for longer than the mind: we may think we have forgiven our parents' trespasses against us, but two minutes under the prodding of a mother's tongue or a father's wit and we find them as unpardonable as ever.

No, there is a better forgetfulness to help the divine mind out of the predicament of its own omniscience. It is the forgetfulness of the dead human mind of Christ. Jesus lay in the tomb—in stone-cold, utter, genuine, human death—from sundown on Friday until sometime before dawn on Sunday. During that time—rather early on in fact—he achieved a state of mind that would have registered as a completely flat EEG: in other words, a state of no human mind at all. His brain was no more a piece of thinking tissue than his leg was a piece of running tissue. Both were mere meat; and neither, left to its own devices, would have been even that for long.

Accordingly, the dead human mind of Christ presents the theologian with a forgettery down which God can drop the knowledge of evil. It is a black hole sucking the things that must not be remembered out of the peaceable kingdom. It is the cosmic garbage can into which the trash of sin disappears. It is an inner darkness that does the work of outer darkness without the theological danger of outer darkness. And it is above all a perfectly dandy place to put hell.

Unfortunately, as I said, this apparently omnicompetent doctrinal concept—this image-of-all-work for the divine forgetting—has one whopping flaw in it: as the Maine farmer said when he tried his first sausage, "It's tolerable, but there ain't much to it once you get it cleaned," so this image says of God that he manages to approve of us only by squeezing practically all the stuffing out of our lives and pushing it to the edge of his mental dinner plate. If my sins and iniquities are remembered no more in heaven, then most of my history stays in the black hole and I come to the supper of the Lamb as hardly more than an empty casing.

On then to the last plank in the last bit of porching: do we have any image that will help us figure how God might actually remember our sins and still not hold them against us? Yes we do.

Every Sunday, when Christians meet, they break bread and drink wine becuase they were commanded to "do this in remembrance of me." Specifically, they gather in special and sometimes opulent buildings—frequently having dressed themselves to the nines—and they proceed, to the accompaniment of expensively produced music and fairly ambitious choreography, to sing and trip their way lightly through the fantastic business of recalling how on a hill far away they once kicked the living bejesus out of God incarnate in Christ. They take the worst thing the human race has ever done and make it the occasion of a celebration. And why? Because the worst thing man did was also the best thing God did. The Friday was Good.

What that suggests to me is that when God remembers evil, he remembers it as we remember the crucifixion in the eucharist: in the light of the good he has brought out of it. And because that is such a hilariously positive good compared to the grim negativity of evil, it simply becomes his supreme consideration. Because of the reconciliation brought about by Jesus' death and resurrection, all our infirmities are made occasions of glory: God just recognizes and remembers them as such. Indeed, if I may try your patience just a little, let me lean a bit on the very formation of the words *recognize* and *remember*. God *re-cognizes* our sins: *he knows them again* from scratch as it were and, seeing us only in Jesus, sees us as his beloved Son. God *re-members* our iniquities: in his divine knowledge *he puts back into a living unity* the broken and dishonored fragments of the lives we lost in death and, holding them as Jesus has re-collected them in his resurrection, clasps us to himself.

But enough of mere assertion. Let me change the imagery a bit and try to nail this final, vindicating plank in place.

fourteen

THE FUNERAL

When I dream, my whole life as I hold it in my own grip is available to me: the events of a party just a few hours ago; the circumstances of a two-week convention six years past; old loves not thought of for years; attitudes toward my father long since suppressed by guilt. But in my dreaming I hold—or better said, I suffer—all those times and places in their unreconciled state. The good things simply rattle around in my sleeping consciousness like so many defenseless beings: really charming people wander off and are replaced by detestable partners; the beloved appears across a room I never manage to traverse; gorgeous views are obliterated by steel staircases and locked doors. And the evil things have free reign: my father hits me in the back of the head; I rage at my children; my friend turns me in to the authorities; I find to my horror that I accidently shaved off my beard.

Do you see? For all the time of my dreaming, what I most ache for, what I most need, is not some vindictive condemnation of those evils, not a vendetta in the name of those goods but precisely a vindication of the goods as they really were and of the evils as the goods that grace can make them become. And when I awake it is just that vindication which, within certain limits, I achieve. Conscious once again—my life held once more in re-cognition by a gracious and ordering mind—I find that everything is now all right: the dreadful shaving off of my beard is held joyfully in the delightful and present possession of my beard; the clip on the head from my father is re-membered in the whole tissue of my relationship with him as the good that he meant it to be in the first place; my own rage at my children is re-collected into the larger whole which is the one thing I meant to matter most; the steel staircases are delighted in as proper steel staircases.

Indeed if what Freud taught us is true, it is only in the re-cognition of those evils that the good can be vindicated. Suppressed or forgotten, whatever good there was in them remains forever under the thumb of evil; it is only in the awake and ordering mind—and above all in the mind that can judge accurately at last—that the things that matter can be seen to matter most. It is not that evil is winked at even for a second; rather it is seen in its true proportion to the good and therefore as not ultimately mattering. We look the betrayal, the cruelties and the twaddle straight in the eye and in that vindicative light of judgment we see them finally as they are remembered in our reconciling, waking mind.

Therefore convert the usual imagery of judgment into the imagery of the dream and watch what happens.

My whole history and the whole of all our histories is held by us as in a dream: the good of it defenseless, the evil rampant. There is for us no gracious and ordering mind capable of re-cognizing it into reconciliation; it remains as we hold it a poor, sad history aching for vindication but never rising higher than poignancy. But when Christ comes to that history as judge he comes as the only awake person in the world, the only one who sees things as they are, who can afford to remember it all, to re-cognize without omission, and so re-collect everything for good.

I think that nails it down fairly well; but before getting off the porch altogether let me tell you a little story that may tighten up the loose ends on the subject of judgment.

Late one evening I was with a group of people who were having an extended series of nightcaps after the funeral of a common friend. We'd all known him well and as the night wore on and tongues got looser the conversation circled back to old Oscar. I say circled back because earlier in the evening we'd regaled each other with a series of fond and complimentary tales about him and then wandered off to other subjects. When we came to him the second time though, someone's casual remark about not wanting to get up the next morning with a big head turned us to the subject of Oscar's drinking. (It wasn't really all that bad; but on the other hand Oscar's liver wasn't all that good, so it got him in the end.)

The fascinating thing about the conversation was that we found ourselves sitting there happily rehashing not only his tippling (we used to find his empties in our desk drawers) but even the resultant liver trouble that jaundiced his whole outlook in the last years. Our first, pious chitchat about his good qualities had, consciously or unconsciously, simply avoided all our most recent experience of him. We'd confined ourselves to half an Oscar—a prettied-up version of a man we all knew to be other, and less, than the one we were praising. It wasn't till the second round of Oscar stories that anyone realized just how fake the first one had been. Suddenly everybody relaxed. We finally had a whole man to talk about and, for the first time, a chance to let the human being he really was rest in peace.

As I think about that night, it strikes me that it provides a handy, if limited, analogue to the day of judgment. First of all, Oscar was really being judged—and accurately. Second, he was being judged in our remembrance—in our re-cognition of him out of the love we all had for him. Third, that love was the overriding consideration: we all wanted a vindication of Oscar, not a condemnation. But last of all, that vindication could not occur until we stopped the pious fakery by which we tried to achieve it earlier in the evening. We really had to judge him—and all of him, good and bad alike—as he really was. Our love could not be operative for him until it had faced the whole man. But once it did, his reconciliation was the most obvious thing in the world. His bad liver and grouchy disposition were no longer a problem for him that night: death had effectively absolved him of all such inconveniences. And in our re-cognizing judgment of him, they were no problem for us either: we were finally free to hold him with all his faults in the proportions our love insisted on. And with no inconvenient, self-propelled Oscar to come around the next morning and bellyache.

Like all analogies of course it breaks down. But even its collapse is edifying: our remembrance of him—our re-collecting word spoken over his history—is not like Christ's. It is not the Word's word with a bark to it that wakes the dead into real resurrection; it is only a human, mental word that does little more than fix up our own insides. But within those limitations it works the same way: it comes to Oscar in judgment out of love; it wills not retribution but vindication; and it achieves that vindication by seeing everything just as it was, but nevertheless re-cognizing it as what our love would have it be. His bad liver isn't forgotten. All the grim days it gave him are known for what they really were. But because they're over now for him, we remember them only under the rubric of the glorious scar: in our reconciling memory, they're held as a funny story about the Boss's embarrassed and totally unconvincing explanation of why empty vodka bottles kept turning up in his trash can.

If Christ's judgment is anything like that at all, it will be— in fact it already is—a great day for the world. It is indeed rigged; but it is rigged only out of love. Even though the fix is in from the start, the fix involves not inattention but the setting of not less than everything in the proportions his love insists upon. But above all it is utterly successful: as Oscar on that evening had no power to prevent his reconciliation in our mental recollection of him, so nothing in the universe has any power to prevent reconciliation by Christ's real remembering of it in the resurrection.

Which is—interestingly and gratifyingly—the very thing the man said:

> For I am persuaded that neither death nor life, nor angels, nor principalities, nor powers, nor things present, nor things to come, nor height, nor depth, nor any other creature, shall be able to separate us from the love of God which is in Christ Jesus our Lord. (Romans 8:38,39)

If now after all that you're still interested in seeing the inside of a doctrine of hell, I think it may finally be safe to sketch one for you. But don't expect me to go back on anything I've said. Any hell we come up with will be nothing more than Oscar, as Christ holds him reconciled, somehow mucking up nothing more than Oscar's enjoyment of the reconciliation. It will be a thoroughly modest proposition: very small, very quiet, and supremely unnecessary.

fifteen

THE DAMN

That last remark about hell's being unnecessary needs, of course, some distinguishing. If, for example, you take it as referring to the fate of any given individual in Christ, it is, by the terms of the gospel, simply true: we are saved in Christ alone who raises us by grace from the absolution of our death; we come before him at the judgment with no handwriting against us. It is simply cheating to say you believe that and then to renege on it by postulating some list of extra-rotten crimes for which Christ has to send you to hell. He, the universal redeemer, is the only judge; as far as he's concerned the only mandatory sentence is to life and life abundant.

Again, if you take the remark as referring to the fate of a given individual as that individual comports himself in the power of Christ's resurrection, then hell is still unnecessary. For if while we held our times here in our own hands, all we had to do to be reconciled was believe he held them in his, how much less will we have to do there when we shall actually see they're in his hands? If we are to find a second death in the midst of such a manifestly reconciled life, we're going to have to go a totally unnecessary billion light years out of our way to avoid the risen nose on our face.

If, however, all of that leads you, as it well might, to ask whether hell is not therefore absolutely unnecessary, I have to hedge a little. For it does have some necessity to it, at least as far as a gospel-regarding theological system is concerned. For one thing the imagery is simply there in the Bible. What you do with it of course is pretty much your own business; the one thing you mustn't do is chuck it altogether.

But there's more necessity to it than that. If you remove the possibility of hell from Christian theology—even out of pure kindheartedness—you do more harm than good: you end up saying that after all the expense and heartache God went through to respect the freedom and integrity of his creatures (heartache for us as well as him), he ultimately reneges on it by forcing everyone's hand, thus turning the whole business into nothing but a cruel charade. Further, you're forced to postulate a God who after all his efforts to persuade his creatures to want what he wants for them, says finally that he doesn't care if they want it or not—a God, in short, who doesn't give a damm about *them*.

But worst of all you come up with a loveless universe. It isn't kindheartedness that makes the world go round, it's love —and if you think they're the same thing you've never been in love. Because if you have, you know that the possible heaven of the beloved's assent to your love comes wrapped inseparably with the possible hell of her refusal. Her response, whatever it will be, is always a staggering mystery, and you invite it only with fear and trembling. Nevertheless, you and I and everybody else who hasn't gone dead or sour go right on inviting it because we recognize our penchant for risky invitations as the best thing about us. All you do therefore if you take the possibility of hell out of your view of the universe is posit a God so interested in playing it safe that he becomes unrecognizable as a lover. The theological function of hell is to be the sacrament of the element of real and ultimate risk by which alone we recognize a world ruled by love. Universalism—as an overriding theological principle— is a false start.

On the other hand, if you ask whether there is in fact a

hell—whether specific persons will actually go so far as to insist on a second death in the face of their resurrection by the supreme Lover himself—that's another matter altogether. And it's one about which I have only four things to say.

First, it's obvious that something like such an insistence is possible in our present state here: nobody, however loved, *has to* love in return. Second, it's manifest from experience that something like it is also actual here: we have all loved people who for a while at least preferred their private hell of rejecting to the heaven of acceptance we held out for them. Third, for the reasons already given it seems necessary to say that such a response is at least possible hereafter. But fourth and finally there seems to be no way of concluding whether it will be actual hereafter or not: we just don't know enough about the mystery of either God's love or human freedom to figure the outcome of a showdown between the two. Moot question therefore. Move on.

While we're on the subject of universalism, however, a few observations are in order. Even as a theological principle, we're not able simply to dismiss it out of hand. For although it can't be made the sovereign consideration (it's only a possible deduction from the doctrine of grace, not the sovereign doctrine itself) something very much like it will be found in every authentic Christian system precisely because it does proceed from the doctrine of grace. To see why, all you have to do is consider the alternative.

Suppose you start out by saying what many people actually think Christianity says, namely, that if you're good you go to heaven and if you're bad you go to hell. Do you see what that does? It voids the work of Christ. The gospel says that it's his reconciliation alone that ultimately matters, that the world the Father loves is the world he sees in the risen life of his only-begotten Son. But if that's true, then he's stopped counting the world's goodnesses and badnesses as the world holds them; he sees them only as vindicated and reconciled in Jesus. If you start counting them again as they are in us, you welsh on the whole idea of Christ alone as the resurrection and the life.

Therefore any authentically Christian system is going to have to keep off the human merit and demerit kick and stick resolutely to a universalism of grace that overrides that subject at least. And they all do—even the ones that at first blush seem not to. Take for example some of the starchily Roman Catholic scenarios of salvation. Historically, they've flirted dangerously with reward and punishment—to the point at times of compromising their Christian authenticity. But where they have not, they've always ended up with a doctrine of hell that paid its respects to the universalism of grace: they've said that the only thing that can put you in hell is final impenitence—an ultimately unnecessary refusal of the free gift of forgiveness in the risen Lord. Sometimes, to be sure, they defined that condition in a way that made it smell strongly of merit and demerit; but insofar as they held to it at all, the hell they propounded was no cosmic inevitability but precisely the weird and unnecessary trick of missing the nose on your face. The exact objection to Romanism that many people have is that it's too easy, that it lets lifelong bounders escape hell just because they squeaked in a confession before they corked off for good—that it acts, in short, as if grace were indeed sovereign and actually free of charge.

Or take Calvinism for another example. At first sight, its doctrine of double predestination (that some go to heaven and some to hell for no reason other than the inscrutable counsel of God) seems light years away from any kind of universalism. But if you look at it narrowly—that is, look only at what it says about the elect who go to heaven—suddenly it's plain, unvarnished universalism all over again. Those in heaven are there on the basis of no merit of their own, and no demerit of their own can keep them out of it. Indeed it is almost a universalism of the worst sort: a freedom-negating, love-denying, drag-'em-in-by-the-hair-of-the-head inevitability. But, for all its defects, it holds inflexibly to the sovereignty of grace and, to that high degree, is authentically Christian.

Somehow therefore whatever we say about hell must be said under the aegis of a universal and effective reconciliation of all things in Christ. If we choose to say *where it is,* it must somehow be inside Jesus' reconciliation. If we choose to explain *how it can be,* we must somehow say that Jesus accepts our willing of it without losing his good will for us. If we want to try to say *what it does,* we must somehow leave it with no detrimental effect on the universal picnic. And if we are so bold as to attempt to say *what it's like,* we must somehow make it even more of a nothing than our first death which is its master image. So much then for the preliminaries. Now for the hell of it all.

sixteen

THE REFUSAL

Nowhere is it more important to work scrupulously from the top. Hell is the ultimate contradiction, the last anomaly, the only holdout from the universal reconciliation of all things in Christ. Therefore it must never be allowed to govern anything. That means in particular that, when our exposition of a given set of theological images is going reasonably well with regard to other doctrines, the fact that it may go badly in respect of hell should not of itself be allowed to spook us into abandoning the imagery. If hell is indeed the only loophole in the sovereignty of grace, it will probably remain something of an exception to any attempt to expound that sovereignty theologically. I realize that sounds suspiciously like stringing a net under a supposedly daring high wire act, but I don't think it is. It's just putting first things first.

From the top then: hell, as I said, is a necessity in any theological system committed to the idea that God loves what he makes—to the proposition that he is not indifferent to his creatures but actually gives a damn what they do with themselves. To put it a slightly different way, it is the inevitable concommitant of the doctrine of judgment that in turn flows directly out of the doctrine of creation: all things are what they are because the Word speaks them into being out of love for the Father. Anything that exists can really be only one thing, namely, *what he says it is*. If he says "aardvark" then aardvark it is; if he says "Zbigniew Brzezinski" then Zbigniew Brzezinski.

But if it is indeed true that human beings can both here and hereafter somehow contradict what he says—that we can counterspeak the Word, as it were, that we can live unreally in the midst of the sole reality we have—then the only verdict the Word can pass on that contradiction is, "That is not what I had in mind at all." Which is literally a hell of a thing to say and, if we were actually to insist upon his saying it forever, would be quite enough hell for anybody—an ultimate failure to know anything, stemming from our ultimate refusal to know the only real self we have to know with. And it would be doubly unnecessary. For in our case he has added to his determinative word of creation an equally determinative word of reconciliation by which he contradicts even our contradictions and holds us justified in his risen life.

Keeping that firmly in mind then, we can attempt to answer some of the questions hell raises. Take for example the question "Where is hell?"

I am aware that most of the scriptural imagery for hell is "separation" imagery: hell is somewhere away from heaven— *out there*, not at the wedding feast of the Lamb; *in darkness*, not in the Light; in a *lake of fire* and a *second death* from which it cannot rise and come back to spoil the party. But scripture also insists that insofar as anything exists at all it exists because of the intimate and immediate speaking of its name by the Word of God. Accordingly there seems to be no way of reading that "separation" as an absolute divorce from God. If we're going to be resolute about putting first things first, then the presence of hell to God has to be the overriding consideration and the separation imagery has to be read as pointing to something other than a merely literal absence from God. It might be read in a subjective sense, perhaps, so that those in hell, even though they're at the party, are there absentmindedly, as it were; or it might be taken in a more ontological sense by which we see them as being there but as perpetually trying to rescind their being by a hassling of the Word who constitutes them.

Therefore the only answer I can give to, "Where is hell?" is to say, "The same place as heaven, earth, and everything else, namely, inside the speaking of the Word." It is nowhere else than at the eschatological picnic where all times are held in the vindicating hand of Christ.

But that of course raises a second question: "Why doesn't hell spoil the picnic? How can you have such a collection of ontological wet blankets around and not have them put a damper on the party?" You note of course that it's a question that doesn't arise if you take the separation imagery more or less literally. Hell, on those terms, is safely *out there* somewhere; there's not even a suggestion of its interfering with heaven—which may be the precise reason for not throwing such imagery away cavalierly. The paradox of hell, as the most contradiction-filled one of all, will in all likelihood be patient of no exposition but the most contradictory. A single, comprehensive insight into the mystery is less likely to be possible here than anywhere.

Nevertheless an answer of sorts can be made on the basis of the imagery of re-cognition: hell doesn't spoil the picnic because as far as Christ and the saints are concerned, they make joyful remembrance of those in hell as Christ holds them in his reconciliation. Even though the damned won't accept that reconciliation themselves, it remains real in Christ: all their evils and miseries are held in him as the only real things they ever can be eternally. If they insist on an everlasting exercise in unreality, that's too bad for them. But it remains an exercise in unreality and so bears no comparison with the overwhelming weight of the real.

That, incidentally, is pretty much the answer of C. S. Lewis in *The Great Divorce*. Hell as he depicts it turns out to occupy no more space at the eternal lawn party than a tiny crack in the ground between two blades of grass. Anyone who wants to come up out of the crack into reality is free to do so; but if he doesn't, he isn't a problem because he takes up so little of all the real "space" available. That has its drawbacks to be sure: it's perilously close to both the imagery of literal separation and the imagery of real forgetting. But it isn't quite the same thing and it may well be the best that can be done.

Still, I'd like to try to press a little harder on my own imagery, namely, that of Christ holding the damned reconciled in his re-cognition of them even while they insist on fooling around with the nothingness of a second death. What does that give you?

Well, to be honest, it gives you problems. It seems to put the damned at the picnic as if they were just so many well-dressed store-window dummies: they're all spruced up and ready for the party but they're not with it. Somehow they're absent from themselves. In one sense of course that's not a difficult image. Everybody's seen it in others and most of use have seen it at one time or another in ourselves: the ten-year-old refusing to enjoy his own birthday party out of pique; the teenage girl having a miserable time at the prom because she's got the sulks.

In another sense however, it's difficult in the extreme: it's a poor party at which the birthday boy is a pill; the prom queen's escort doesn't have much of a time if she keeps grouching all evening. It's hard to see how you can have the damned as large as life at the eternal party and not have them slow the proceedings considerably. After all, since it's their whole life that's present there—and not only present in Jesus himself as he holds them but present in all the others they ever had to do with (because Jesus holds them too)—it would seem hard for those others to have their old buddies around when the personal response that's the one thing they most want from them is not about to be forthcoming. The

imagery of re-cognition worked nicely with Oscar on the evening of his funeral, but chiefly because Oscar wasn't able to
walk back in and obtrude his recalcitrance on our joyful
remembrance of him.

What do you do with it then? Well, I think the only thing
is to acknowledge that when you try to use the imagery I've
been working with to answer this second question, it begins
to break down. You can save it only by shading it in the
direction of C. S. Lewis: the damned are at the picnic but
they don't spoil it because somehow they're not there as
large as life. They can be thought of as there only in two
ways: first, in Christ's remembrance of them, in his effective,
joyful re-cognition of all things; but second, in their own vain
remembrance of themselves, that is, in a second death in
which, like Oscar in his first death, they're not sufficiently
with it to interfere with the festivities.

But that in turn can be made to work only if you do one of
two things: either you read their remembrance of themselves
into smallness—into a crack in the ground or a darkness outside; or you take it as a retreat into a kind of self-absorption
that effectively precludes their having any adverse relationship with the party—into an insistence on knowing something that's no longer there to know (namely, their life as
dead) and that's therefore incomprehensible to any real
knower. In Christ's re-cognition and re-collecting of them
they remain as large as his grip wills them to be—and *that*
knowledge of them is available to the saints—but since they
insist on only their own grip, since all the agency they will to
exercise at the party is the agency only of a dead hand, they
obtrude themselves on the party as no more than the dead
nothing which is all their grip can be. Like Oscar, they don't
make waves.

If you find that a bit tortured and want to go back to
straight separation imagery, I can't blame you. The re-cognition plank, inside the house of hell here, doesn't look like too

solid a place to put your foot. Still, if you're in the theological building trade you just keep on hoping that it won't collapse completely. Two more questions therefore and we're at an end.

Given the imagery so far, wouldn't it be wiser to say that we make our own hell and not get into the business of having God damn us? If he wills life and life abundant, why should we set up a system in which we obscure that truth by having him somehow will the utterly contradictory second death as well? The question obviously is, "Who wills hell?"; and the answer I think has to be, "Both God and man." If you want to make a nice canned theological distinction, you say that the *proximate* and *effecting* cause of hell is man's will, while the *remote* and *enabling* cause of it is God's. God makes hell possible but not necessary; man unnecessarily makes it acutal.

It remains important, however, to steer clear of the flatfooted assertion that hell is nothing but a subjective state of our own devising—that God has no relationship to it and no particular feelings about it. Those in hell are as much the apples of his eye as those anywhere else; if they are so cantankerous as to refuse to see that, then God can only look on them forever and stamp his foot. He just has to say, "Oh, damn!" If he can't get mad, he's not much of a lover. His wrath, to be sure, is vindicative, not vindictive; but precisely because it's nothing other than his love in the face of contradiction, he wills it in the same act by which he wills his love. And therefore he wills hell simply by being unwilling to stop loving. No doubt annihilation would make for a pleasanter situation; but that apparently is not one of his options. Reenter here therefore all the imagery of the worm that dieth not and the fire that is not quenched, of weeping and gnashing of teeth—none of which is a bit too strong for any lovers' quarrel, let alone an eternal one.

And that brings you to the last question: "Is hell eternal?"

The Bible of course says rather plainly that it is, and most theologians who've taken scripture seriously have said the same thing. A few, like Origen, have been moved by the vision of the sovereignty of grace to postulate an eventual closing up of the infernal shop; but up to recent times the church has almost too enthusiastically acted as if hell would be in business forever.

My own answer to the question is, "It all depends on how you set it up." Nowhere more than in answering posers like this is it obvious that theology is a game: about the facts, nobody knows anything; therefore all we do is juggle our own perceptions. Here are mine:

Grace is forever sovereign, hell is forever unnecessary: as far as anyone now in time and space is concerned, we believe that he can avoid hell simply by believing the gospel of grace. The question therefore comes on the condition of those who have passed from time to eternity: can those who enter eternity having refused to believe Jesus' gracious reconciliation ever take back that refusal? Can there ever be a "moment" or a "point" in their eternal contradiction at which they get fed up with their stupid sulking, look finally at what Jesus has in hand for them and with a huge, sheepish, all-relieving grin just cut out the nonsense?

As I said, it all depends on how you set it up. The usual answer (namely, it's impossible for that to happen) is based on a sharp distinction between time and eternity: time, being a succession of moments, allows you to choose something in one moment and unchoose it in the next; eternity, being one single unending moment, leaves you no such room to maneuver. Eternal choices therefore can't be rescinded.

If, however, you make time and eternity less mutually exclusive, the usual answer doesn't have to be given. Watch.

Time (along with space) is a condition of creation as we hold it in our hands; eternity is a condition of that same creation as it is held in Jesus' hands. Accordingly, all moments in time are held, as we've said, for our eternal exploration of them. Therefore even though the damned are deeply committed to only the most unreal exploration of those moments, the real moments themselves are always there in Christ and it is at least possible for any or all of the inhabitants of the lake of fire to take a fresh and refreshing look at them. The way is open for them on, say, their nine millionth unreal re-collection of the day a redwinged blackbird flew across the gray sky or the time the beloved's eyes shone purple in the sun, suddenly to catch on to what it was really about and blow themselves right out of the fiery drink with one huge laugh at all their fuss over nothing.

Set it up any way you like therefore. Better yet, decide which answer you like best and rig the question so you get it. As long as you don't throw out any images, there's no reason why theology shouldn't be pleasant.

FALL
—
HEAVEN

seventeen

THE IMAGERY

I make my last transition without tricks. In place of all the theological fancy dancing I did on hell and summer, let me just set before you the images of that happier mystery in which it's always autumn.

For on no subject more than heaven is it so essential to remember we don't know beans about the reality. But then, happily, on no subject is it safer to let our minds simply play with the images: since no figure however florid can possibly do justice to the facts, not even the plainest, crassest image has to be ruled out of the game. And since the invitation is indeed to play, no gambit—not even the old, disused opening of literal interpretation—is necessarily against the rules. Let us play, therefore, with:

The new heavens and the new earth

The holy city, new Jerusalem, coming down from heaven prepared as a bride adorned for her husband

The marriage supper of the Lamb

The wiping away of tears

The making of all things new

The city that lieth foursquare

The building of the wall of it of jasper

The city itself pure gold like unto clear glass

The twelve foundations of precious stones: jasper, sapphire, chalcedony, emerald, sardonyx, sardius,

chrysolyte, beryl, topaz, chrysoprasus, jacinth, ame-
thyst
The twelve gates that are twelve pearls, every several
gate of one pearl
The street of pure gold like transparent glass
The light not from sun or moon but from the Lamb
himself
The river of water of life
The tree of life whose leaves are for the healing of the
nations.

Do you see? When *we* speak of heaven, we make it a
spiritual bore—so much so, that *heaven* is almost the least
useful word we have for talking about it. When the New
Testament speaks of it, however, it makes it an altogether
earthly riot of richness, color and kindly light—an autumnal
spectacle in which town and country, earth and air and light
and water appear at their ultimate, transfigured best. Like
the season it steals a page from, it looks a lot like home: time
then to head for heaven and fall.

It is September 10th. The leaves are as green as summer
ever saw them, the garden even lusher and more demand-
ing. The squash bugs have long since triumphed over the
zucchini, and the flies that have survived till now seem fit
enough to elude the flyswatter forever. The thermometer is
pushing 90 degrees. Mothers are fanning themselves at the
stove. Children, confined in totally glassed-in schools, are
frying in their own fat. And yet everyone is happy.

Why?

Because it's fall, that's why.

"Ah, but," you object, "fall does not begin till the equinox.
This rejoicing is only because it's still summer."

Wrong. Summer ends, as everyone knows, on Labor Day.
Solstice and equinox may mark the boundaries of other sea-

sons but in the case of summer we shorten the hellishness of it all not only by terminating it before its time but also by ignoring the actual date of its start. We do not pretend for example that winter begins on the first Monday in December or ends on the first Monday in March. Nor do we delay the advent of spring until the celebration of a Grand and Glorious Fourth of April. But with summer we are more than content, as creatures made in the image of an intelligent God, to have it begin late and end early: the less of it the better. Of the four seasons therefore it is only of fall and spring that we desire to have more.

But as I was about to say before you interrupted, what is there about fall—about even early September's faked-out fall by anticipation—that can take circumstances indistinguishable from summer and make them occasions of joy? How is it that autumn can drag us through hell and still make it seem like heaven?

It is because autumn has a future.

"Ah, but," you object again, "considered in terms of its ultimate destination, fall has in fact less of a future than any season. How can the prospects of waning light and increasing cold be causes of happiness?"

False question. Admittedly if fall's prospects were as you describe, they could indeed cause only misery. But they are precisely the reverse. We expect confidently and correctly that fall will bring us, if not a greater *quantity* of light, nonetheless a *quality* of it that is absolutely great for living in: low, long light—and reflected everywhere in burnished reds and golds. Likewise we cannot properly be said to expect increasing cold: that is winter's outlook. What we in fact look forward to in fall is decreasing heat: balmy coolness made all the more welcome by the knowledge that with each additional day the likelihood of our escaping the fire of hell steadily increases.

In fact in the further wisdom of the race we have installed

within the heaven of fall itself the only tolerable version of summer known to man—and certainly the only version whose coming we so desire that on the least pretext we announce its arrival before it gets here. I speak of course of Indian summer: that choice center cut of the year, that filet of the prime season itself when all the hell that tormented us in its own time is re-cognized (oops! jargon; sorry, blame it on hell) and re-membered in the high time of autumn. Indeed if only the Holy Spirit had seen fit to include Indian summer among the images of scripture, we might never have had so much trouble reconciling heaven and hell.

But as I was saying: fall has a future and we find ourselves brightened by it because like all true futures it does its gladdening work by suffusing the present with hope. It does not hold itself out to us simply as some other, better day that may eventually arrive; it informs today with the very reality it represents.

And what is that reality precisely?

It is the fact of renewal.

Please do not interrupt to tell me fall is not a time of renewal.

First, think of children. Even though they find it *de rigueur* to proclaim their hatred of the opening day of school, they actually love it. It is the first time in months that they have experienced something more than the pure, soul-deadening immediacy of summer, the vacancy of vacation, the tedium of time that is only today, the hell of a futureless existence. And even if, in a week or a month, the bright future that fills the start of school is replaced by merely present failures and frustrations . . . still, while it lasted they were almost human again. And why? Because they felt that something new was not just coming but in the works.

Or take ourselves. Summer is drift. The whole world is either out in the Hamptons, out to lunch, or both. Consider for example my own chosen line of work. The only thing in summer worse than being unable to get your editor on the phone is actually catching him in. Irresolution, thy name is Publishing in August. Nothing can be done, you will be told, because Arthur's sailing on the Sound, Phyllis is lost in the woods and Irving's canoeing across Canada. The whole industry is off on an expensive, vain pursuit of a renewal that will be delivered to its doorstep free for nothing in four weeks. Hang up and call back in September.

But the best proof of autumn's power to renew is a fact I've already mentioned: by the beginning of fall the seeds are already formed, the buds are already in place and the young of animals are strong enough to winter through till breeding time in spring. The future of every living thing is already here, held proleptically under the riot of color that is autumn. And the precise hope nourished by that future is the hope that the new order thus dazzlingly held in germ and sperm will be not some strangely other dispensation but this same old lovely order itself triumphant on the other side of winter's death.

As a matter of fact it's always seemed to me that the colors of autumn, far from being just a circumstance of climate and chemistry, a replacement of chlorophyll by xanthophyll, are in fact *mating* colors: the signals of a transcendent sexuality by which the late November actually even goes the disturbance of the spring one better. Just as the males of certain fish—stippled darters, redbelly dace—take on billiant hues at spawning time, so in fall nature itself (indeed *him*self: this is Father Nature) romances the dark time of the year before inseminating it. Spring may strike the note of sex; but it's fall that rings the cosmic changes on our chimes—and with rebirth, not just birth, as its theme. Even if we didn't have heaven to pair it with, autumn would still speak plainly of the greatest mystery of all.

Shouldn't we find it odd then that we haven't allowed the spectacle of fall to shed more light on heaven? Having all but been hit over the head by a paradise on earth, shouldn't it seem peculiar to us that when we talk about paradise itself we go out of our way to make it sound as unearthly as possible? Shouldn't we ask ourselves where our penchant for making earth and heaven totally discontinuous came from?

Yes we should.

And kindly refrain from telling me you rather thought there was supposed to be a discontinuity between them.

Almost everybody thinks that. The world to come as conceived by the popular imagination is grossly irrelevant to this one. It is a vaguely benign future condition in which human beings (who have by then ceased to be human and become pseudo-angels with paper wings and tin halos) sit on clouds (of uniform, unvarying whiteness) and play small harps and lyres (both of which instruments the race early and wisely retired to the closet). It is a picture of a quintessentially mind-numbing experience—not to mention its being an image that utterly denies the body. The first man was of the earth, earthy; but in this thin and vaporous heaven of bed-sheeted intelligences there is not one man's leg, not one girl's knee, not one baby's bottom. It is a dismal downsitting underpinned by nothing at all.

And from where, pray tell (besides from the bottomless pit) does the imagery of such anti-bodies come?

From scripture, you suggest?

Well, there are some who think it does. Like the woman who said on noticing that her neighbor's Santa Claus had only *four* tiny reindeer, "Well, if people don't read their Bibles what can you do?" there are those who firmly believe that the word of God is a treasure trove of such vapid, spiritualized nonsense. They have apparently either not read or not noticed scripture's plethora of choice, autumnal images, all of which are earthy to the point of excess: new skies and new earth; a new Jerusalem (which, when you think about it, is no less earthy than a new Bronx would be); and all the unnecessarily gorgeous colors of its walls, its gardens and its gallant walks. But then, I gave you all that.

No, the dumb imagery—the pictures that bespeak no connection between this old autumnal beauty of a world and the glorious world to come—is not from scripture. It's from a rotten religion that says that earth is a nasty place where creatures do piggy things and that no self-respecting Supreme Being can afford to allow even a scrap of it in his nice, antiseptic heaven. It's from people who hate creation, not from a God who loves it.

But since the dumb imagery has often been advanced by vocal and otherwise intelligent people (rotten religion knows no bounds), it has insinuated itself not only into the mind of the masses but into the thinking of theologians. The great temptation in theology is to think that high-sounding abstractions tell you more about God than simple, earthy images. In reality of course neither tells you a thing about him as such, and both give you only analogies and hints at best. Still, given a choice, the average theologian, like the average person, chooses to ignore the images and go with the abstractions. Watch for example what that preference can do with the phrase "the world to come."

As you know, in its common acceptation it is a synonym for heaven. Accordingly, in ordinary usage it comes to share all of that concept's bloodless unreality. It is almost as if the word *world* were not even in the phrase. The amount of carryover from this world to the next that is allowed for in most people's theologies is nearly nil: our (presumably) spiritual minds may get into the world to come; but neither our physical bodies nor, God forbid, any of their earthly circumstances or parameters are to be given a heavenly home. And that leads straight to the idea—to cite just a single commonly held theory—that in heaven there will be no time. Because the next world is eternal (whatever that means—it's a cinch nobody who ever talked about it really knew), these theologizers conclude there is no room for past or future there, only for a present.

The idiocy of that conclusion can be manifested either from experience or from scripture. Permit me to display it from both.

First, from experience. If there is a heaven worth talking about it will be a nice place (if it's not we should be whistling in the dark, not doing theology). And if it is indeed a nice place, the only kind of niceness it makes sense for us to predicate of it is human niceness (any other kind and we're talking through our hats). Now then. Of all the aspects of this life that are capable of introducing niceness into our days, none is more effective than a future that can suffuse the present with hope. And likewise nothing so robs life of any niceness at all as does the conviction that we are going nowhere. Even going to hell in a handbasket is more interesting.

Accordingly, when theologians expound heaven as a state in which everything is simply present and nothing at all is future, they deserve all the yawns they get. The image immediately conjured up in every sane person's mind is that of Sunday afternoon as a child: Daddy is asleep, Mommy is dozing over the crossword puzzle and there will not ever as long as you live be anyplace to go again at all. It might be sold as a halfway decent picture of hell of course; but then, such theologians never were any good at recognizing a chance to make a buck.

Finally, from scripture. Not only has the "world" in "world to come" been ignored for no good reason, the whole idea of time has been run off the eternal ranch in spite of the fact that all along it was a "time" word that lay at the heart of the Greek version of the phrase. The "*world* to come" in Greek is the *age*, the *aeon* to come. *Forever* in Greek is not some futureless eternity stalled in an endless present but a glorious going somewhere, a moving from time into still deeper time, a progress *to the aeon, into the aeons, unto the aeons of aeons*—which last phrase, please note, the old translators had the wit to English as *world without end*.

Amen therefore. Do you see? Our ages, our times, our seasons—like our hands, our eyes, our limbs, our whole world—all go home in the resurrection. The next world is none other than this world, next. As there were futures here to suffuse a meager present, so there will be risen futures there to transfigure a glorious one. And as there were pasts here to be researched by memory, rummaged through by dreams and re-called by love, so there will be risen pasts there held for our endless exploration.

Judgment, like spring, declares what God had in mind; heaven, like autumn, insists he's got it all in his pocket.

eighteen

THE STORING

It's October 14th. For a week now the temperature has been dropping to 50 degrees or lower overnight, so the ground is cooling fast. That, combined with this morning's moist, 65-degree air, gives you patchy fog on the golf course and grass that's wringing wet. I lower myself gingerly to lie down on the fairway but the minute my back touches it, the chill comes straight through my shirt. I spend a long minute warming up the earth.

At 7:20, the southering sun is barely up, but its effects are spectacular: the fog is a transfigured white, and great horizontal shafts of gold shoot through the corridors between the patches. I feel like a recumbent Charlton Heston in a Cecil B. De Mille towel opera.

Bible clouds, my children used to call these epiphanies: God putting the golden finger on the world. I wonder: what do kids use for religious imagery now that no one has old illustrated Bibles around? I grew up on one of those. The best picture was The Rebellion of Korah, Dathan and Abiram. I can see it now: the three Levites, plus two hundred fifty men with censers, plus wives, children, dolls, dishes and furniture, all being swallowed up by a crack in the ground as wide as the Missouri while Moses has God illuminate the scene with enough searchlight beams to open a shopping mall. Come to think of it maybe the kids are better off without all that. We put the finger on ourselves quite nicely, thank you: there's no need to dragoon the kindly light into doing our dirty work for us.

I run home, split some wood and head into the house through the garage. On my way I take a chicken, some sausage and a couple of pounds of butter out of the freezer. Supper. But before I close the door, I look. There in front of me are shelves of frozen tomato Purée, blanched zucchini, mashed butternut squash, chopped Swiss chard, stewed eggplant, sliced beets—not to mention bagsful of basil, sage, dill and coriander. You name it, we grew it; and a good two-thirds of it we processed. Furthermore, next to the freezer there's an old refrigerator of my mother's. That's full too: it's wall-to-wall pickles, mincemeat, chutneys, conserves and marmalades (we don't exactly *can*, you see—at least not by the water-bath method—we just put boiling stuff in boiled jars, screw on the lids, then cool and refrigerate: works fine).

It's a lovely sight though, and it suggests a comparison: on the golf course the sun's shafts shot out at me from the sun itself; here in the garage they shine on me out of all the things the sun has stored itself in. The days may be getting shorter but the light has gone inside things. We'll have it all winter no matter how the sun may hide.

Come to think of it, even the woodpile is stored light. Wood's expensive now, and since I try my best to heat only with found wood, I don't usually have all that much of it on hand: just a porchful, if I'm lucky. But some day if my ship ever comes in—or better said if a rich uncle ever leaves me three thousand acres of Maine woodlot—I'm going to build something I haven't made in years: a Polish woodpile. (I think that's the right name—at any rate I saw my first one up-island in Yaphank where there were a lot of Polish farmers. Where's "up-island?" Oh. That's confusing: it doesn't refer to this island. Yaphank is on Long Island itself which, compared to Shelter Island, is the mainland. Since the natives here are purists though, they never call it that. Everything west of the other side of the ferry—even Brooklyn if you please—is "up-island" from here. Also, while I'm making things imperfectly clear, let me stuff one more item into this parenthesis: strictly speaking you never make *a* Polish woodpile; they come invariably in twos).

Anyway, what you do is draw a circle twenty-five or thirty feet in diameter on level ground. Then you lay down a first course of split wood (cut to stove lengths) so that the outer ends of the pieces just touch the inside of the circle all around. Then you lay additional courses on top of that one, setting the outer edge of each course back an inch or so from the outer edge of the one below it (what you're doing of course is tapering in the whole pile so that when it's finished it will look like a giant beehive). When you've gotten these courses up to a height of about two feet, you lay down a second, inner circle of pieces snug up against the first and you build that one up too. After that all you have to do is keep going till it's the height you want. (You can make it look fantastically neat if, after you've finished laying a course, you go around the pile with a small sledge hammer and tap the pieces three courses below into perfect position.) In any case, before you top it off—or maybe even right as you build it up—it's a good idea to fill up the empty space in the center by tossing in junk wood. To any child the temptation to play inside an empty wooden igloo is irresistible: you don't need a lawsuit charging you with maintaining an attractive nuisance.

As I said though they come in twos: you start your first one at the end of one winter and you build your second during the next: one pile's always coming down and the other's always going up. Admittedly, you may find you have photographers coming and going as well: not everybody can provide the sight of a pair of substitute suns in his yard.

And the city had no need of the sun, neither of the moon, to shine in it, for the glory of God did lighten it and the Lamb is the light thereof. And the nations of them that are saved shall walk in the light of it; and the kings of the earth do bring their glory and honor into it. And the gates of it shall not be shut at all by day: for there shall be no night there. (Rev. 21:23–25)

You know something? I've written and preached for a good many years now on the kindliness of the light who is the Lamb of God. And do you know what thanks I've gotten for telling people the good news that on the youngest day Jesus, the *Phos Hilaron*—the *gladsome*, even *hilarious light*—will speak well of them? Very little. They resent being told they don't have to make a big fat effort. Firmly convinced that their own bootstraps are the only way up, they either accuse me of universalism, immorality and indifference, or else they subject me to a barrage of questions about how it can possibly be—as if what was promised by Jesus in the Gospels and spelled out by the Holy Spirit in the rest of the Bible couldn't be true unless I could explain it and they could understand the explanation.

But now, even though nobody needs it and hardly any of those self-improvement mavens deserves it, I just may have hit on the image that does the trick. We're all fit for the city of God for the same reason that the squashes and the eggplants and the firewood are fit for the city of man: *the light goes inside*. Whether it's Jesus or the sun, when it shines it not only flatters but transforms. If we don't want to believe that, of course, we can all go to hell. But it remains true nevertheless, and the whole of the hell we go to will never be any bigger than the nail hole in Jesus' hand or the spear wound in his side: even if we won't say yes to the light inside, we stay smack inside the light himself all the same:

In him was life and the life was the light of men, and the light shines in the darkness and the darkness can never take it down. (John 1:5)

Therefore as in autumn we gather in the things that have stored up the light and been made glorious by it, so in heaven God gathers us:

For God who commanded the light to shine out of darkness has shined in our hearts to give the light of the knowledge of the glory of God in the face of Jesus Christ. (2 Cor. 4:6)

But we all, with open face reflecting the glory of God are changed into his very likeness from one degree of glory to another. (2 Cor. 3:18)

Self improvement indeed! Tell that to the woodpile.

nineteen

THE POIGNANCY

November. Indian summer has come and gone, and with it the last of the lush images of autumn. This is now fall in earnest: all the trees bare now except for a few yellow flags on the maples and the crisp, sere leaves on the piss-oaks that will rattle all winter in the wind.

The gardener has stopped counting the frosts and just keeps mental track of the order in which he knows the garden will succumb. Everything's gone now but the late-planted mustard greens, snow peas, Chinese cabbage and kale—and the perennial herbs that never got taken in. As the cold deepens all of that will go too, in just about the order given. Only the kale will winter through for sure. The herbs may or may not make it: at this latitude you take your chances with them unless they're planted right up against the house. Should've potted them up for house plants. Maybe next week. Right now it's hard to work up much enthusiasm. The whole place is mostly just forlorn-looking, just . . .

Poignant . . . that's the word. When I first got the idea of tying heaven to autumn, I wondered a bit about whether I could bring it off after I got to late fall. Everybody has a pretty fair grip on the cheerful imagery of September and October, but in the long run it's the dour image of autumn as end that has the real grip on us. How's it going to be possible, I asked myself, to take a time of the year whose final note never gets any higher than poignancy and use it as a paradigm of hilarious triumph and roaring success? How, in other words, get to a happy eternal wrap-up from a season whose conclusion looks only like loose, lost ends.

Well, as I said, it's a poor theologian who can't make a buck by reversing field and turning his problem into a solution. If you can't figure out how earth's lost ends can point to heaven, you turn the whole thing around and try explaining how heaven can deal with earth's lost ends. In other words you stand the question on its head and ask how God manages to remember all the untidy terminations we've strewn behind us in this vale of forgetfuless and still not have them mess up his eternal housekeeping. Above all, you inquire how we who have survived here mostly because we got away from those bitter endings can possibly flourish hereafter in a state where they all catch up with us.

People think hell is a difficulty. They worry about whether it exists or how God can put up with it or why it doesn't spoil heaven. That's all nothing compared to the real problem: why doesn't *heaven* spoil heaven? It's the folks inside the new Jerusalem who have the toughest hash to settle. If you've been on the outs with your brother for twenty years and you go to hell, what's new? No matter whether he gets to heaven or not, you can go right on ending your relationship with him forever. But if you've made an earthly career of not speaking to your ex-wife and then the two of you end up in heaven . . . boy, have you got a problem! Boy, has God!

But to see just how big the problem is you have to hunt around for an ending here on earth that's a real sockdolager of a finale, not just a temporary cutoff. And in spite of what you might think, there aren't all that many to choose from. Take fall, for instance. It can be as sad and final-seeming as all get out; but one straight look at the seeds on the dill or next year's buds on the rhododendrons and the whole thing is practically a joke. Or take human relationships that come to nothing. Take marriages that end because of death or even divorce. Sure, a lot of it stops; but a lot lives on too: in children and old friends, in holidays and memories—even in furniture and flatware.

No, in all those endings there's still more than enough material for recall, remembrance and recogition. It's only a small step therefore from the images conjured up by that material—by, say, the evening with the photograph album or by the lock of hair that reminds you of the three-year-old your estranged daughter once was or by the sudden realization that the quarrels were all a ludicrous mistake—to the image of a heaven where the same joyful recollection takes place on a grand but ultimately uncomplicated scale.

What we need therefore is an image darker than any that death, divorce or December can provide. They may end lives, relationships and seasons but that's all they end. *They still leave a world behind them*. And because the world left behind held, and was held by, a vast web of persons—because it was a tissue of relationships here—when God raises it hereafter he brings both them and it into the greater web of glory.

Is there, accordingly, any end we can find that finishes off not only the relationships between people but also the whole universe they shared? Can we think of a termination so thoroughgoingly final that it will aggravate our theological problem to the nth degree and leave God with a world that apparently nobody knew except the people who shared it—and that they themselves, by their own catastrophic choice, now refuse to remember?

There is indeed such an end. And anyone who has been through it will think of it all too easily. Is it the breakup, in both sorrow and anger, of the clandestine love affair shattered by betrayal.

Consider first what such an affair creates. The lovers, from the moment they first acknowledge their love and through all the years of its flourishing, bring into being a secret world.

Small matter that they live at the same time in the broad and common world we all share of PTA meetings, supermarket parking lots, hotel lobbies and city streets. To them, their traffickings among those things become not a private, partial world naughtily excised from this one but an integrated and integrating wonder that makes this world into the very catholic whole it never was before.

Music I heard with you was more than music
And bread I broke with you was more than bread . . .

They become the defining conjunctions, the very knots of a web of light into which all the old world's threads are gathered in glory:

Oh, there will pass in your great passing
    Little of beauty not your own,—
Only the light from common water,
    Only the grace from simple stone.

Consider next, though, how the end comes to what once was so plainly world enough and time. Pass the details of the treachery—whether he strayed or she, whether with one or with many, whether mindlessly or in full advertence; and pass all the questions of who was guilty of what—of whether the sinner failed in justice or the sinned-against in mercy. When a world ends there is no point to postmortems: there is a bomb; there is a button; there is a finger: and then there is nothing. The question of why it happens collapses at the feet of what occurs. Consider that alone.

Their whole world existed only in the secret interchanges of their love. Publicly it was shared with no one: at meetings they sat on opposite sides of the room; in the lobby of the Algonquin, they sipped an afternoon vermouth like cousins. And privately all the physical evidence of it perished: there were no gifts given that would last longer than a sprig of honeysuckle, no snapshots taken that could be preserved even outside an album, and nothing written at all that could be kept. They even made light of their destruction of evidence:

> Lives of great men all remind us,
> As we o'er their pages turn,
> That perhaps we leave behind us
> Letters that we ought to burn.

But as a result of all that care to appear nowhere as they really were and to leave no memorial of what they had in fact done—when at last, in short, whosoever finger it was actually pressed the button—the bomb had to do no more than to end their conversations in order to end their world. It was necessary for them only to hang up when they heard each other's voices on the phone. The rest was silence—because there was no rest at all:

> Spring will not ail nor autumn falter;
>   Nothing will know that you are gone . . .

In better days they had recited the rest of the stanza for each other:

> Saving alone some sullen plough-land
>   None but yourself set foot upon . . .

But at the end there was not even that. They had sworn never in thought, word deed to revisit their past. Nothing survived the vow.

Now I think you see the problem: God knows their past whether they want him to or not. And more than that, he

holds it reconciled in Jesus for their exploration: not only
does he have the private world they once knew but he also
has the public, eschatologically manifest world that his sovereign remembering of it insists upon. But how then can he
have them in heaven—how entertain them at the supper of
the Lamb, at the final eucharistic recalling of every world
that ever was—when they themselves refuse to recognize the
one world by which they best knew all the others?

The answer of course is that if you put the question that
way, God can't. There are only two ways in which it is con-
ceivable that God can get his eschatological druthers with
them: either he leaves them in the hell they've so obviously
shut themselves up in, or else they stop shutting up and start
talking to each other in the heaven of a world he's got prepared for them.

But since only the second of those alternatives has any
likelihood of making a salubrious autumn of their fatal fall, let
us ignore the first and try simply to imagine what they could
possibly have to talk about as they gather up their lost ends.
Let us ask the last question: of what must they make remembrance and re-cognition, what is it that they must re-call
and re-collect (no apologies; it is the last time) when they
finally decide to share an eternal afternoon vermouth?

Clearly they must speak of the whole tissue of their relationship as Jesus has spoken it into reconciliation. All the
good years, all the days of wine and talk and books. And all
the elations of their exchanges: the Vivaldi, the autumn
woods, the laughter on the bed of leaves and the stillness
after long love. And the thousand elegies before death that
were the counterpoint of their desire:

There will be rose and rhododendron
    When you are dead and underground
Still will be heard from white syringas
    Heavy with bees, a sunny sound.

Still will the tamaracks be raining
  After the rain has ceased, and still
Will there be robins in the stubble,
  Brown sheep upon the warm green hill.

But then, all the betrayals too. All the missing of each other's meaning ". . . that is not what I had in mind at all . . ." down to the last treachery, unnecessary and inexorable, by which the knots of light were undone and the threads of their world raveled into nothing. Of all that must they make recognition if they are to reenter the city of their love as Jesus holds it for them. The years of lost worlds and dead love must be recalled—in the Lamb of God who died and lost a world too but who rose again and fetched it back—as the only thing they can possibly be forever: glorious scars, spear wounds in the side of love's risen body, nail prints in the hands that hold all of history in remembrance.

I know. If here in this life you have ever known such a world's ending as I have described for these two lovers, you can see no earthly way for it to become a world's beginning hereafter. All I can say is that I feel that too. Our ultimate reconciliation in heaven remains the tallest of all orders; it remains a mystery; and in the light of our unre-cognized history until now, it remains inconceivable even as a possibility. But then it never was presented to us as such. It was announced as a fact accomplished without our cooperation by a grace unconditioned by our concurrence.

"No man can know or feel he is saved; he can only believe it." At the end of the game of images we put the cards back in the box and go to bed with nothing but the trust we started with. Another hand perhaps in the morning; but through the dark night, only faith.

THE LAUGHTER

Allow me a penultimate image, though, before we finally put the lid back on the card box. The moonstruck terms in which I've just expounded the eschatological reunion of two adult delinquents raises a quite natural question: what in heaven, pray tell, are their respective spouses—those long-suffering saints who spent their earthy days gagging on the antics of this pair—supposed to be doing while the lovers get their act back together for eternity? Is the theologian able to propose nothing better than an everlasting hard swallow for the bystanders, innocent or not, of such romantic reckless driving?

No doubt you recognize that question as a minor variation on the worst poser in all of Christian theology. Permit me simply to state it for you in its most extreme form. It is: what in heaven are six million Jews supposed to be doing while Hitler makes his peace (a peace, please note, that has been prepared for him regardless of whether he makes it his own or not) with some blond, blue-eyed Aryan he had an earthly falling-out with over the mismanagement of a death camp?

I have no intention of answering the question in that form. Theological chitchat, even correct theological chitchat, about the ultimate acceptability of what is now clearly and totally unacceptable can only seem impudent. There lies—indeed there *must* lie—at the bottom of every good Christian stomach the hard, indigestible lump of God's obscenely poor judgment in pardoning grave sinners. So much so, that in the eternal reconciliation he is probably going to have to ask for, and we are certainly going to have to grant him, pardon for his Divine Bad Taste. Back therefore to the less offensive variation on the problem.

Once again, to see the answer you must aggravate the question. Indeed, if you will cast your mind back, you will see that I have already made a start at just such an aggravation: I postulated treachery in our two lovers' putative affair. I need do no more now than extrapolate that to treachery in spades. Let me supply them accordingly not only with spouses but, as the result of divorces, with several spouses each (they were after all anything but international grand masters at the management of abiding relationships). And since I postulated betrayal as well, let me assign them additional partners in hanky-panky—additional clouds of witnesses, as it were, to their inability to remain content in any one bed for long.

Now I think you begin to see how all those witnesses might surround them on their eternal afternoon. To help him with his joyful recognitions, for example, there will be three wives, five mistresses and fourteen more-than-passing acquaintances; to jog her risen remembrances, two husbands, three lovers and twenty-seven playmates, none of whom she ever allowed to get to first base. Think of the insights to be gleaned from notes compared! Imagine the leaps and bounds of self-realization made possible by comments delivered! "That's our Al, all right: Monday, one woman kept happy in the bedroom and four amused from the phone booth; Tuesday, three in the sack and two on the wire. Hard to tell who he did better by, Simmons or Ma Bell." Or, "Listen, Freddy. Don't complain. With Gloria, even if you got to first, she could always manage to throw you out at third."

And think of the introductions, not to mention the responses: "Myra, this is Pauline. She was the four business trips to Kansas City." "It's good to meet you, Pauline. You're prettier than I imagined. I must've had you mixed up with that Paulette who was the $1200 incomprehensible over-charge from American Express." Or: "Ralph, this is my husband Harry. You know something? I almost got the three of us together on October 19, 1964, but luckily I managed to find the back door." "Pleased to meetcha Ralph. I always wondered why you had such a draughty house."

Once again—if you will pardon a small presumption—it's close to what the Man himself actually said:

> Ye do err, not knowing the scriptures nor the power of God. For in the resurrection they neither marry nor are given in marriage, but are as the angels of God in heaven. (Matt. 22:29,30)

Do you see now the last image of all? It is the image of the family reunion long years after the old relationships of superiority and inferiority are over, after proprietorship has died and risen again as friendship. It is the picture of the hilarious dinner party where grownup children recount how they pilfered their father's wine as teenagers—and where grownup adults answer them not with penance, counsel or absolution but with smiles. In the peace that passes understanding, everything beforehand turns out to have been only misunderstanding. The eternal afternoon's awkwardness gives way to grace, and the evening of everlasting laughter begins.

EPILOGUE

In all seasons, after my morning run, I perform a ritual. Rain or shine, snow or sleet, I am invariably dripping wet, so I remove my perspiration-soaked shirt and undershirt and prepare to throw them down the cellar stairs for laundering. The throw however is anything but a mindless toss: I try my best to make them land not on the steps or on the floor but on the banister only—and precisely at the newel post if at all possible. And why do I put so much effort into so simple a task? Why do I stand in the cellar doorway frantically putting body English on a couple of soggy shirts? I will tell you why. It is because under all my Christianity I am a pagan at heart. I am convinced that if I land the shirts properly, the day will go well: the otherwise surly powers of the universe will have been induced to smile on my projects. But I am also convinced that if I do not, my personal world will come unstuck: I have made a religion, you see, of taking off sweaty clothes.

You are no doubt disposed to find that a silly business—an exercise that can have no more effect on reality than stepping on a crack has on your mother's back. I agree with you. But I would also like you to see that the ineffectuality of such rituals is not the real root of their silliness. They're foolish not because they're the wrong tool for the job of jimmying the universe into line but because the job has already been done by Jesus. Indeed, thank God they *are* the wrong tool: if the likes of us really had the power necessary to straighten out the world, we'd make it a bigger mess than it is. What I want to do here at the end of this book therefore is simply to set these pointless religiosities of ours in the light of the reconciliation freely given to us on the youngest day and—if nothing else—laugh at them for the right reason.

You may have wondered why in a book about the four seasons and the four last things I have so carefully avoided any mention of the liturgical seasons of the Christian year. One reason is simple: the subjects have been linked that way before; I wanted a fresh approach. But the other reason is more complicated.

In the long run, Christianity is not a religion. While it uses the forms of religion—while it has observances, days and seasons that seem to be intended to fix up our relationship with God and the universe—it is in fact the announcement of the end of any need for such influencing at all. It is the proclamation of the gospel that God has fixed up everything himself and it is an invitation to believe that incredibly cheerful piece of good news.

Accordingly, were I to have carried on about the rituals of Advent and Lent, of Easter and Pentecost, I would have led you astray. For these observances are of no more value religiously than is my tossing of sweaty clothing. They are celebrations, and earthly celebrations at that (the best things about them happen in kitchens, not churches) of a reconciliation already accomplished. They are emphatically not transactions by which God is conned into being nice.

Religions, from the point of view of the gospel, are useless. And their uselessness is rooted not in the truth or falsity of their tenets or in the effectiveness or ineffectiveness of their rituals but in the very fact that they are religions at all. It lies in the profound stupidity of two assumptions that they all make and that I've already alluded to. The first is that after Jesus there is still something that needs effecting before the human race's problem can be solved. And the second is that we could actually effect it if only we had the right kind of whammy to put on the problem.

Which is why I brought up my basement banister religion. The real objection to it is not that it can't work but that I shouldn't be standing there acting as if there were a need for it to work. It's bad news not because I've got the wrong religion but because I've got any at all. I don't need to run around looking for the right recipe to save the world, because even if I found it I'd still use it wrong.

The real criticism of all religions—of the false ones that tell you that chicken sacrifices or occult phenomena or astrology or futurism can save the world, and of the true ones that tell you morality or humanitarian values or scientific knowledge can do the job—is one and the same. True or false, all such instruments are in our hands. Whether they can actually exercise a controlling effect or not, our exercise of them is never under control. In our grip, their results are invariably less than hilarious.

It is only in some better grip therefore that the world can be saved. It is only in some other hand far removed from the uselessness of religion that the work of religion can be accomplished. It is only in short on the youngest day—in the hand of the vindicating Word—that laughter can ever be restored to the world.

But because that laughter is already a fact just on the other side of death, it is also already a fact just on the other side of our unbelief. We are asked to believe not that our reconciliation will be true some day but that it is true already and that we are invited *now* into the hilarity of it all.

But in Christ, the whole cloth of our dayes has been made seamlesse againe now, and woven from the top throughout now, and made white in the blood of the Lamb now. Go now therefore to that Lamb. Go not to those things *propter quae venit ira Dei super filios in-credulitatis, on account of which the wrath of God cometh upon the children of unbeleefe;* but go onely to him and go onely by beleeving. For his wrath cometh upon all men who in their incredulitie seek to stand (whether in innocence or in guilt) upon those things. But it cometh upon no childe of beleefe, if onely he confesse that he is dead and his life is hid with Christ in God. *Nihil ergo nunc damnationis; there is therefore now no condemnation* to them that are in Christ Jesus. We are saved by a free and boundlesse gift, and we are saved now. For now is the accepted time, now is the day of salvation, and now is Christ risen from the dead and become the firstfruits of them that slept, if onely now we will beleeve. Therefore *to day if you will heare his voice,* to day he will heare you: . . . he can bring thy Summer out of Winter, though thou have no Spring; though in the ways of fortune, or understanding, or con-science, thou have been benighted till now, wintred and frozen, clouded and eclypsed, damped and be-nummed, smothered and stupefied till now, now God comes to thee, not as in the dawning of the day, not as in the bud of spring, but as the Sun at noon to illustrate all shadowes, as the sheaves in harvest, to fill all penu-ries, all occasions invite his mercies, and all times are his seasons.